The Mystery o[f]

'Maureen began to climb but gave up half way and let herself drop down.

'How on earth do you do it? That rope is really hurting my hands.'

'Hand over hand,' explained Teddy. 'Use one, then the other and go quickly.'

Maureen tried again, but just as she had once more reached the half-way mark a voice came from below.

'What do you kids think you're doing? Are you trying to break your necks? Get down at once.'

Maureen released her grip on the rope so suddenly that she went tumbling down the side of the tower, landing in a heap in a patch of nettles. . . .'

But why is the grumpy stranger so interested in the round tower? The McDonagh children decide to find out, and soon find themselves involved in another mystery. . . .

Jo Ann Galligan

The Mystery of the
Lost Tower

Illustrated by Terry Myler

HAWTHORN BOOKS

The Children's Press

For Tom

First published in 1986 by
The Children's Press
90 Lower Baggot Street, Dublin 2

© Text Jo Ann Galligan
© Illustrations The Children's Press

ISBN 0 947962 07 7 paperboards
ISBN 0 947062 08 5 paper

Typesetting by Computertype Ltd.
Printed in Ireland by Mount Salus Press.

Contents

1 Cloigtheach Mhilic   7

2 The Old Map   21

3 The History Room   30

4 The Mill   41

5 The Secret Room   51

6 Caught!   61

7 Into the Tunnel   72

8 Mystery of the Round Tower   87

   Notes for Teachers   94

   Author   95

1 Cloigtheach Mhilic

Kevin McDonagh tossed a handful of blackberries into the pail which his friend Liam was holding for him, then swung himself down carefully from the hawthorn branch, avoiding the thorns which studded it.

'I've had enough!' he declared. 'Between the hawthorn and the blackberries, I'm in shreds. I'm going back to the house to do my homework.'

'What have you to do?' asked Maureen. 'I thought you'd finished last night.'

'I had, but I still have my drawing to do. We're doing a project on Meelick and I have to draw the round tower. How am I supposed to do that? I've never been there, and anyway I'm useless at drawing. It's my worst subject.'

'Never seen the round tower?' echoed Liam. 'But you've lived here all your life.'

'We've driven past it lots of time,' said Teddy, 'but we've never stopped. It's funny, we've been to several others like the one at Turlough, but somehow we've never been to Meelick. I suppose we thought it was so near we could go there any time.'

'Well, if Kevin has to do it for Monday, I think we ought to pay it a visit tomorrow,' suggested Liam. 'Why don't we take a picnic and Kevin could sit there and do his sketch? The weather's still good enough for us to go on our bikes.'

'Okay,' agreed Teddy. 'One o'clock at the mart. We'll bring drinks and sandwiches. Can you take apples?'

'Sure can!' Liam nodded. 'Dan's trees are covered this year and I can bring half a dozen each if you like.'

'Are you off, Liam?' asked Maureen.

'If we're going out tomorrow, I'll race off home now. Dan has a few spuds left to dig, and if I hurry I can get finished and be free tomorrow. So long!'

'Bye!' shouted Kevin. 'Don't be late meeting us!'

'And don't forget my apples!' added Teddy.

The three McDonagh children made their way in the opposite direction, back across the fields to the house. Although it was well into autumn, the day was warm and still and the children were still in summer jeans and tee-shirts, their bare arms well scratched by the brambles. The air was so still indeed that even the poplars surrounding the McDonagh ' land had stopped their usual rustling. Carrots, Kevin's dog, was lying in a sleepy coil under one of the trees, and he dragged himself lazily to his feet as they neared him.

'Carrots is too tired to wag his tail!' announced Teddy. 'It's too hot to work at all. No wonder I'm exhausted!'

'Back already?' called their mother as they picked their way wearily through the garden and around the side of the house. 'Oh, that's great! You've plenty of blackberries picked. What's the next plan?'

'A rest!' exclaimed Kevin. 'We're off to Meelick tomorrow. I have to do a project on it for homework, so we have decided to go out on our bikes.'

'That sounds like fun. You'd better check your tyres so — didn't you say you had a slow puncture, Teddy?'

'Oh, sugar! So I have. Come on, you two, you can give me a hand to mend it!'

Despite the puncture, and the subsequent panic when

8

Teddy thought he had a second one next morning — only to discover that he had not adjusted the valve correctly — they left the house on schedule and were at the mart in plenty of time to meet Liam.

'How far is it?' asked Kevin, drawing level with his friend as the latter freewheeled up to them and they continued on out of Swinford town on the Castlebar road.

'A couple of miles,' he answered. 'I've been out this way loads of times on foot, but this is my first time on a bike. It takes just under an hour walking, so we should bike it in fifteen minutes.'

'Dan was great to let you have the bike, Liam,' said Maureen. 'Doesn't he use it himself to go in to Mass?'

'He went early when he realized I was going to something educational later!' chuckled Liam. 'He's all for seeing me catch up with the school work any way I can! I don't mind myself when it involves a trip like this. Can't say I'm so keen on the book learning part of it!'

Liam's parents were travellers and he had attended school from time to time in various areas, but had never spent long enough in one town to master anything more than the basic skills of reading and writing. However he was a clever boy, and now that he was settled for the time being with his farmer friend Dan, the old man he had come to regard as an adopted grandfather, the Vocational School had accepted him as a first-year student. Here Liam was learning carpentry and metalwork — which he enjoyed — as well as maths and English, which he tolerated! His spare time was spent helping Dan, in exchange for his keep, and learning how to care for Dan's prize ponies.

'Doesn't seem to be an educational trip, at least not to

me,' said Teddy. 'Going for a bike ride and then having a picnic while Kevin draws his pictures is my idea of a day off!'

'What does the name Meelick mean?' asked Kevin. 'I could put that in my project, couldn't I?'

Maureen braked slightly, allowing her bike to lose speed until Kevin had drawn level with her.

'It means a low-lying swamp. I expect the land around there was all under water in the old days when the weather was bad. Some of it is still pretty swampy. We'll be able to see the tower soon, over on the right beyond the railway line.'

'It's got another name too,' called back Teddy unexpectedly. 'Some people call it *Baile an Tuir*. That means Steeple Village.'

'I thought you weren't getting involved with anything educational?' pointed out Liam.

'Oh, well,' conceded Teddy modestly, 'got to pass on my knowledge to the younger generation, haven't I?'

As there were exactly two years between Teddy and his younger brother, Liam burst out laughing at this remark.

'You poor old man! You'll be wanting a walking stick yet!'

'Race you!' was Teddy's reply and he raised himself up from the bicycle seat and began to pedal with all his strength. Liam rose to the challenge and a few seconds later the two older boys had disappeared round a bend in the road. Maureen and Kevin followed at a much slower pace. Kevin was enjoying the feel of the breeze on his bare legs. Soon, he knew only too well, the shorts and tee-shirts would be packed away on the top shelves and out would come the winter jumpers and boots. Kevin spent as much time as possible out of doors, either digging in his little corner of the garden, or perched in the tree-house Teddy had built, a pile of books or comics close at hand. In the winter, in Kevin's opinion, far too much time was wasted indoors.

'Is that the sign?' asked Kevin suddenly, letting go of the handle-bars and pointing. Ahead of them was a white sign, outlined in green, which said *Cloigtheach Mhílic*, and beneath this the legend in English, "Meelick Round Tower".

'Right on,' agreed Maureen. 'Put your hand out to the right, silly, to show you are turning that way.'

As Kevin swooped sideways towards the tower road, Maureen followed a little more cautiously and the two of them set off up the side road after the others.

'It's only about a mile up here,' said Maureen. 'I remember coming up here once with Dad in the car. You come to a sign with a squiggle, to warn you about a hill, and then there's a lot of twisty bits. We might have to walk some of that if it's as steep as I think. Then we come out of the scrub on to bare road again, go by someone's farmyard, and the tower should be just ahead on the right.'

Green trees and bushes rose on each side of the road here and the lingering autumn warmth made the rich scent of ripe blackberries hover around them temptingly.

'I'm getting hungry!' said Kevin. 'Wouldn't mind stopping for a few of those berries. Aren't they huge? They're far better than the ones we picked yesterday. Should have come up here in the first place.'

'They might not be so good if they grow right on the roadside,' replied Maureen. 'Fumes and things from the

11

cars, you know? We could end up with petrol jam!'

'I don't think it would make any difference, Mum washes them anyway, doesn't she?'

'That wouldn't take away the pollution. It would be right inside them. I wouldn't eat them, for one.'

'I would,' said Kevin cheerfully. 'Oh, look, there's your sign now. The Sign of the Snake-like Squiggle! Watch out for reptiles in the undergrowth!'

'Idiot!' laughed Maureen. 'It doesn't mean snakes, you ignorant child! It's the sign I told you about, the one that tells you to look out for turns and twists in the road.'

'That's what YOU say!' retorted Kevin. 'I happen to know. Beware of snakes, that's what it means!'

'There are no snakes in Ireland,' pointed out Maureen. 'Didn't you ever hear tell of St. Patrick? He banished snakes from Ireland.'

'These are immigrants,' answered Kevin seriously. 'You know the circus that was playing in Swinford a week or two ago? Well, these snakes were performing there and they decided to stay. The circus people couldn't find them so they stuck up a notice to warn people and just left them to it!'

'Anyway, there's the hill ... and it isn't as steep as I thought. I think I'll manage. You go first. We'd better stick to single file here in case a car comes. These corners are tight enough.'

'Agreed. Over and out,' and Kevin cycled on ahead, occasionally standing on the pedals to give himself more impetus.

Before long they had come to a section of the road where the border growth became shorter and more sparse, then finally petered out. Visibility was better here

12

and Maureen drew level with her brother once more.

'You can feel it colder here,' she remarked. 'It's amazing how warm it is between those hedgerows ... oh, look, there's the tower now.'

He looked across the fields in the direction she had indicated, and caught his first glimpse of the tower, just the upper half, which stood out above the rolling grassland like some prehistoric rocket.

'It's amazing,' she continued. 'I didn't notice it so clearly when we came that time in the car. How lonely it looks, all by itself, sticking up in the air.'

'There's the farm coming up now,' said Kevin. 'Good! I'm going to have my lunch before I do any drawing. That was a long hard ride.'

'There are the others now. Look ... sitting on the wall.'

Ahead of them now was the neat stone wall on the hillside which surrounded the graveyard. In the midst of the tombstones towered the monument they had come to see, and right in front of it sat Teddy and Liam, their backs towards the tower, munching on some sandwiches.

'You could have waited for us,' called Kevin. 'Greedy pigs!'

'Is that all right, eating beside a graveyard?' asked Maureen anxiously. 'Don't you think it would be more proper to have our food on the road?'

'We're not in the graveyard, only on the wall,' explained Liam. 'And we're not doing any harm, are we? We'll gather up all the papers and things after.'

'I'm not moving,' put in Teddy. 'I'm perfectly comfortable where I am. If you want any you'd better hurry up, before I eat everything!'

Kevin propped his bike against the abutment wall and

13

swung himself up beside the two older boys.

'Here's my contribution. Mum sent some buns. Maureen has bottles of squash.'

'It's amazing, isn't it?' observed Liam, looking at the tower. 'How on earth did they get all those stones up to the very top?'

'There's a story that a witch took them up in her apron...' began Kevin, but he was howled down by the others.

'Not that old story again!...'

'Don't they tell the same story about every round tower in Ireland?...'

'You didn't get THAT one from the teacher!...'

'How did they build it then?' asked Liam.

'I reckon they had wooden scaffolds,' said Maureen, 'and as the tower got higher, the scaffold around it got higher too. Then when the building was finished they knocked the scaffold down again. That's what Dad thinks, anyway.'

'Sounds logical enough,' agreed Liam. 'They certainly didn't have cranes in those days.'

'There's another way they could have done it,' said Teddy. 'Maybe they had a stone staircase running up the inside of the tower, and they used it for lifting materials up. The higher the tower grew, the higher the staircase would be. They built it all together, you see.'

'They didn't have staircases,' scoffed Kevin. 'We already did that in history. They went from one level to another with ladders. There was a hole in the floor at each level for the ladder to poke through.'

'Well, that blows away my theory,' said Teddy. 'The scaffold must be the answer so.'

'Scaffold or no scaffold, they must have been pretty strong to carry some of those stones,' said Liam. 'Look at the size of some of them. I couldn't lift them, let alone carry them to that height. And how did the scaffold take the weight?'

'It's a problem,' drawled Teddy prosaically, 'but not one that I am going to let interfere with the task in hand — which is feeding me! Now, Liam, how about some apples?'

Liam dug into a plastic bag and produced several small green apples.

'Here you are. These are the nicest of all. Everyone goes for the big red ones, but these are much sweeter. Dan and I had four each last night, they were so juicy!'

Kevin stood up. 'I feel better now. I'm going over to have a look!'

There was a notice on the west side and Kevin read it aloud. Here on the hill top his voice carried down clearly to the others and even Teddy stopped munching for a moment so he could hear.

A monastery once existed here but its history is not known. The only remains of the monastery are the gravestone with the inscription OR DO GRICOUR, A Prayer for Gricour, and the Round Tower. These Round Towers were used as belfries or as places for refuge in time of danger, and were built in the period 900–1200.

'What's a belfry?' asked Teddy.

'A belltower. The Irish word *Cloigtheach* that we saw on the signpost means bell tower.'

'I wonder who Gricour was?' asked Kevin. 'Poor old

Gricour, lost and forgotten hundreds of years ago, I expect.'

'He isn't forgotten,' Liam pointed out. 'You've just remembered him.'

'He might have been a monk when the monastery was there,' suggested Maureen. 'Or a priest. Or just an ordinary farmer from the parish.'

'Here's the gravestone,' called Kevin, continuing round the base of the tower. 'It's stuck up against the side. That's a funny place to be buried.'

Maureen joined him. 'That wouldn't have been the original grave. Look, it's fixed against the side of the tower with metal clamps, and that's modern concrete behind it. It must have been flat on the monastery floor at one time, and when the remains were being preserved they stuck it here where people could see it more easily and it wouldn't get damaged any more. Gricour is probably buried somewhere else, with a new grave stuck on top of him.'

'Poor Gricour,' repeated Kevin softly. 'I wonder what he was like?'

'He must have been quite important,' said Maureen. 'Look, this gravestone must have been beautiful when it was first made. It's got all sorts of decorations and crosses all over it. You can only just make out the *OR DO* bit.'

'Well, I think that's a super way to be remembered,' said Teddy. 'When I'm dead I hope someone puts a monument to me up against a round tower, and in a thousand years' time people will be saying, "Oh, look! Pray for Teddy! And who, pray, was Teddy? Well, he must have been a great fellow to get himself left in a place like this. And look at the lovely decorations, and what sort of fellow do you think he was"…'

'You have no respect for anything,' laughed Liam. 'Now, what do you think our chances are of climbing inside the tower to have a look while Kevin sits down and does his sketching?'

'There's a rope hanging down this side,' said Teddy. 'Someone else must have had the same idea. And look, there are spikes sticking out of the side. We can climb up as far as the door.'

'Do you think that rope has been there since the tower was built?' asked Kevin.

'Of course not! That's been put there recently. As for the spikes, they are just big bolts.'

'I'm going to try and climb up,' announced Liam. 'Stand back! If I fall and hit my head on a gravestone that will be the end of me!'

The doorway to the tower was a good ten feet or more from the ground. Once, when the tower was used as a refuge in times of war, the monks would have climbed up by ladder and then pulled it inside the entrance. Nobody could then climb up after them without being firmly discouraged! An old wrought metal door, held at one side by two hinges, hung drunkenly open.

Liam was already half way up to the door. An iron railing hung outwards and as he neared the top he took hold of it to steady himself.

'Be careful!' warned Maureen. 'That door might be all rusty. It might not take your weight at all.'

Liam tested it carefully. 'I think it's sound. I'm going to swing myself up now. Hold your breath and cross fingers!' and with that he drew himself up on to the sill. Here there was a ledge about three feet deep and Liam could sit comfortably on it.

'What can you see?' called Kevin. 'Is it dark in there?'

'Not completely. There is some daylight coming through from the top of the tower where the roof is missing, and I can see the opening where a ladder would have gone through to the next level. There must have been a cellar room below this one at one time.'

'A dungeon!' intoned Teddy mournfully.

'Well, the floor is nearly all fallen in now,' explained Liam. 'You can see where it was though. It was level with this door at one time.'

'Stone floor or wooden?' asked Maureen.

'Stone, I guess,' replied Liam.

'Yes,' volunteered Kevin. 'We did that at school as well. It was a stone floor, made of lots of stone slabs lying on their sides and pressing against each other. It was called corbelling.'

'Why didn't all the stones just fall down?' asked Teddy.

'They did!' was Liam's answer. 'There are only one or two left in position now, so there you are!'

'I hope you're safe up there,' said Maureen anxiously. 'What if something else falls down?'

'It's stood here long enough,' said Liam. 'I would say the outside is safe enough. Look at those huge foundation stones,' and he pointed down to the base of the tower. Sure enough, a circle of huge dressed stones, as regular in appearance as modern cast concrete blocks, encircled the tower base, and these in turn rested on further large slabs of stone.

Below that, nothing was visible, as the grass had grown up in a thick mat, but here and there a lump of stone rose up out of the greenery.

'There could be several feet of foundations for all I know,' added Liam, 'but you can be sure it would have caved in long ago if it wasn't well supported.'

'Do you know anything about the foundations, Kevin?' asked Maureen.

'Not much. We didn't do a lot — we're to do more after we have the drawings finished. But the teacher did tell us there wasn't a lot known about what was underneath. I know, because I asked if there were any dungeons and she said that as far as she knew the only cellar part was the room under the entrance door. And that would still be above ground level, wouldn't it? The other thing she told us was that this tower was repaired — about a hundred years ago.'

'Do you suppose we are allowed to be climbing up like this?' asked Maureen suddenly. 'We might get into trouble for defacing a monument or something!'

'Can't see why we shouldn't,' replied Teddy. 'We're not doing any harm after all, and besides, if we fall, that's our own affair!'

'I suppose you're right,' conceded Maureen. 'We're here for educational purposes anyway. Kevin, why don't you get your picture drawn and then we will have done our duty.'

'Right on!' agreed Kevin in a mock midwest American accent, and drew a crumpled notebook and pen from his pocket. He stepped back several yards from the tower, just missed sitting in a huge blackberry bush, and sank down on the grass to begin his masterpiece.

'I'm coming up too,' said Teddy. 'Move over, Liam. There's room for me up there too, isn't there?'

'Come on,' answered Liam, 'but don't push me.'

Teddy shinned up quickly and the two boys stared down into the depths of the tower. Heaps of broken stones and twigs were the only remains of centuries of debris. A broken eggshell lay forlornly in one corner.

'Jackdaws,' commented Liam. 'They must have built a nest and it all fell in.'

'There might be bats too,' added Teddy hopefully. 'All tucked up and fast asleep on the sides of the walls up there.'

'Possibly,' agreed Liam. 'It would be a good place for bats. Nice and high!'

'Come on, you two,' called Maureen. 'I want to go up too and I can't get up until one of you comes down.'

'I'm coming,' said Teddy, and taking hold of the rope he swung himself down like a real acrobat. Maureen began to climb up but gave up half way and let herself drop down again.

'How on earth do you do it? That rope is really hurting my hands.'

'Hand over hand,' explained Teddy. 'Use one, then the other, and go quickly.'

Maureen tried again, but just as she had once more reached the half-way mark a voice came from below:

'What do you kids think you're doing? Are you trying to break your necks? Get down at once!'

2   The Old Map

Maureen released her grip on the rope so suddenly that she went tumbling down the side of the tower, landing in a heap in a patch of nettles and just missing a large stone which reared up beside them.

'Are you all right?' enquired Teddy anxiously. 'Nothing broken?'

'I'm all right, just stung.' Maureen rubbed her hands together ruefully. 'Good, there's some dock. Just as well I was wearing jeans or I'd have been well blistered!'

While she was examining her hands the man who had shouted up to them had managed to get the wire off the entrance gates and let himself in. He came dashing up to the foot of the tower, leaving the gate wide open.

'You heard me! What do you think you're doing, climbing up there? Kids aren't allowed to climb that tower!'

'There was a rope,' said Teddy defensively, 'so some-one must have been up before us.'

'That rope has no right to be there either! Dangerous, that's what it is. You could do a damage.'

'We weren't doing any harm,' piped up Kevin. 'Only having a look. I have to draw the tower for my homework and anyway you could have killed Maureen shouting like that!'

'And serve her right. She had no business up there. You don't climb up again, do you hear?'

'We hear,' said Teddy. 'Look out, mister, or you'll be the one that's hurt!'

The man followed Teddy's gaze up. A pair of trainers was hovering just below the ledge of the door, and then a pair of legs followed.

'Another one? How many more of you are up there?'

'Just Liam,' said Kevin. 'Here he comes now,' as Liam swung down as expertly as Teddy had done.

'I know you! You're one of those tinkers that were here last summer. What are you after in the tower? There's nothing in there for the likes of you.'

Liam stared coolly back at him. 'I don't think that's any of your business. How do you know I'm not working for the Board of Works?'

The stranger was taken aback by Liam's answer; he had not expected to be challenged in this way!

'Just clear off, you kids. I'll be back later to make sure you're gone.'

With that he turned and went back to the gate. Half way there he stumbled in the uneven ground and nearly went sprawling. Teddy stifled a giggle.

'Serve him right, the grumpy old eejit! Getting over the wall wasn't good enough for him, he had to be posh and go round the long way!'

'He's dropped something,' observed Liam. 'Looks like money. We'd better get it and give it back.'

'Bad luck to him!' declared Teddy. 'Let's keep it. Damages for Maureen's nettle stings!'

'Can't do that,' protested Maureen. 'Come on, let's get it.'

She picked her way downhill through the uneven ground and bent down. 'It isn't money, just an old bit of paper.' Cupping her hands, she called down to the man, who was now getting into his car, 'Hey, mister! You dropped this!'

If the man heard her he gave no answer, just slammed the door and started up the engine.

'Hard luck,' said Teddy. 'You tried. How much is it? A fiver?'

'I said, it isn't money,' repeated Maureen. 'It's a photocopy of something.'

'Let's see,' said Liam, peering over her shoulder. 'Oh, it's in Irish. I can't read that.'

'That isn't Irish,' contradicted Teddy.

'Latin, I think,' said Maureen. 'We'll take it to Dad. He'll know for certain. They all did Latin in school in his time.'

'I think we should go now, before Grumpy comes back,' suggested Kevin. 'I've finished my drawing,' and he held up a rather lopsided sketch with one window too many.

'Yes, let's go home,' added Teddy. 'I have a feeling — and only a feeling, mind! — that we are about to fall into another Adventure!'

'What rubbish!' scoffed Liam. 'People don't just go round having adventures.'

'We had one already this summer,' declared Kevin. 'And we solved it, didn't we? We got the Westport cross back and helped the guards catch the robbers!'

'Just luck and being in the right place at the right time,' said Liam. 'I wouldn't count on any more now!'

'Race you back to the main road, Liam!' challenged Teddy, swinging himself over the high wall and down to the road. 'Now, how come my bike wasn't waiting for me? If that was a horse it would be standing there ready for me to leap into the saddle!'

'You watch too much TV,' said Maureen.

'I'm an all-action man,' replied Teddy, ringing his bell loudly. 'Sling down that there supply sack, Kevin. I'll get a head start on those varmints!'

Liam was right behind him as he sped round the corner, and Maureen looked at Kevin and shrugged. 'Looks like we're left behind again. I suggest we go out through the gate. That man left it wide open and cattle could get in.'

'For a man who was worried about us harming the tower, he certainly acted funny,' observed Kevin.

'What do you mean?'

'Well, if the gate is normally shut so cattle can't get in, wouldn't you think he would have been sure to stop and see it was closed properly? Why worry about us? Cattle would do far more damage than a few children.'

'Yes, you're right! Why didn't I think of that?'

'Oh, you would have done,' grinned Kevin generously. 'My opinion is: He knows something about the tower that we don't, and he doesn't want us to find out. And I think that piece of paper has something to do with it.'

Maureen spread out the sheet. It was quite small, a jagged corner from a photocopied sheet. There was a rough compass sketch in one corner, and, top centre, a circle was outlined, together with odd lines and crosses. The rest of the paper was covered with a florid scrawl. The original had obviously been badly creased for parts of the scrawl were almost illegible.

'If it does, Dad will know. Let's go. I don't want to meet Grumpy either,' she finished. 'We've done what we came for.'

Later that evening the four children lay on their stomachs in the McDonagh's living-room, the paper spread out between them. Teddy had unearthed a Latin dictionary from among his father's old schoolbooks, and Maureen had pen and paper ready to write down their conclusions.

'The first word is *Sub*. Something to do with submarines?'

'This paper must be older than submarines, silly. It's a photocopy. The original could be hundreds of years old.'

'There's a funny squiggle here. Perhaps it's meant to show water,' suggested Liam. 'These squiggles could all be water. It might be a river or a lake.'

'What's that you have?' came the voice of their father from the doorway. 'Playing Scrabble?'

'No, it's just a bit of paper,' said Kevin before the others could stop him. 'There's a kind of poem on it, but we can't understand it. Then there are a couple of words in English.'

'Let me have a look,' said Con. 'Yes, it's a kind of map. Did you have this photocopied? It looks as though it's quite old, although someone obviously added the English bit at a later date.'

'Yes, it's a copy,' put in Maureen quickly, before Kevin admitted that it was not they who had had the copy made.

'It's a map of a building, as far as I can make out. There's a Celtic cross at each end of the sketch so it must be a church or something like that. Do you want me to translate?'

'Can you understand it?' asked Liam, impressed.

'Some of it, anyway. The first bit is easy. *Sub* means under, and the first three lines are *sub aqua, sub terra, sub turre.* That means *under the water, under the ground, under the tower.'*

'Under the tower?' repeated Teddy.

'That's what it says. The next part isn't quite so clear. It looks like *a-u-r-u-m* — that would be the Latin word for gold. The word beside it is difficult to read. The original must have been folded just here. I think it's *c-e-l-* at the beginning. It could be *celavi.* That would mean *I hid.'*

'I hid the gold,' repeated Maureen. 'Yes, that could be it. What do the other two lines say?'

'*Fidelis* means *faithful.* That word is perfectly clear, but I can't make out the next one at all.... It's a blur.'

'What's the last line?' asked Kevin.

'*Ubi flumen* and then another blur. *Where the river* is the meaning of that bit.'

'Can you read the English bit, Dad?' asked Kevin.

'Let me see now. There's somebody's name — O'Keefe — and a date. 1883 is it? It's hard to tell.'

'What could that mean?' asked Maureen.

'I would imagine it refers to the person who drew the map,' explained Con McDonagh. 'Or, of course, it could be a book reference. You could find that easily enough. Where did you get this anyway? It looks like an old parish map to me. If it is authentic it must be very old.'

'Oh, I didn't get the original,' said Liam innocently. 'It just turned up.'

'Kevin's doing a project on the round tower at Meelick,' explained Maureen. 'He came across this while he was doing his research.'

'Putting in some old legends are you, Kevin?' asked his father. 'That's a good idea. Makes it more interesting.'

The children gave a sigh of relief as Con went out. Now they could read the map in peace — and they had the information they had wanted without having to compromise themselves! The three McDonaghs began to talk at once, but Liam called for order.

'Let's take things one at a time! First of all, let's write the English translation down before we forget it.'

Teddy produced a felt-tip pen and Liam began to write slowly and carefully beside the Latin poem:

> *Under the water, under the earth, under the tower*
> *I hid the gold,*
> *Faithful ... where the river ...*

'That makes a sort of sense,' observed Teddy. 'Perhaps the missing word is something to do with finding it ... the gold.'

'Of course!' said Maureen. 'Meelick was sacked by the Normans and the monastery was split up. Perhaps one of the monks had some treasure and he hid it before he left.'

'Yes,' agreed Kevin. 'And he left the map as a clue, and then Grumpy found it, and now he is trying to get the treasure.'

'It does rather look like we've found ourselves another mystery,' decided Maureen. 'This is great!'

'What if it isn't the round tower at Meelick?' exclaimed Teddy suddenly. 'There are hundreds of towers in Ireland, aren't there? It could be any one of them. It doesn't actually say here that it's Meelick, or even Mayo.'

'We won't be doing any sleuthing next Saturday, anyway,' said Kevin gloomily. 'We have to go down to Attymachugh. Dad promised Uncle Ed he'd be down with his new cabinet, and we're all invited for the day. It

28

will have to be Sunday afternoon again.'

'In the meantime,' suggested Maureen, 'why don't we go over to the library and see if we can trace the book the map comes from? If Dad is right and "O'Keefe" is a book reference, we should be able to find it quite easily.'

'How do we get to Castlebar?' Liam asked. 'School doesn't get out until nearly four. It would be too late to go over then.'

'We get out at three,' said Teddy, 'and if we go straight there we'll have at least an hour and a half till closing time.'

'My teacher lives in Castlebar,' said Maureen. 'If she would give us a lift over after school, we could get a ride back with our neighbour. He works over there, and comes back every evening.'

'That's perfect,' agreed Liam. 'I won't be able to come, but anyway you can read faster than I can!'

'How do you find out where a page comes from?' asked Kevin. 'There must be millions of books in the library.'

'There's probably a card index of subjects,' said Maureen, 'but in any case, we can ask at the desk. I'll see my teacher tomorrow and ask if she can take us over on Tuesday. You can see Bob about getting back home, Teddy. And we'll meet here on Tuesday night to decide where we go next. All right with you, Liam?'

'Fine by me. I'll be off now so.'

'Wouldn't it be marvellous if we found a new tower full of treasure!' Kevin's voice was wistful. 'We'd be famous ... really famous.'

3   The History Room

'Where to now?' asked Kevin, looking up at the library building. 'It's a lot bigger than the library in Swinford.'

'Castlebar is the county town of Mayo,' explained Maureen, 'so all the important historical stuff and things like that get stored here. They have to have a big place to put all that in.'

'Come on,' urged Teddy. 'The sooner we go in, the sooner we'll get what we want. I've got our map here.'

The boys trailed in after Maureen and they looked around the room, trying to locate the reception area.

'There, in the corner,' whispered Kevin. 'There's a girl we can ask.'

'Hello,' said Maureen, smiling brightly. 'We want to look up a map in one of your books. How do we do that?'

'Do you know who wrote the book?' asked the girl. 'Then I can tell you if we have it here.'

'It might have been written by someone called O'Keefe,' offered Teddy.

'Title?'

'We don't know,' said Maureen, 'but it could have been a history or geography book. Can we find it out that way?'

'You can, of course. I have the card index right here on the desk. We'll see under Geography first, shall we?'

She shuffled through the cards while Kevin, an ardent reader, stared in fascination. 'Can you really find out that quickly?' he asked.

'Of course I can. With all the books we have here we'd never find anything if we didn't have a reference system. Every book has a number printed on the spine, you see, and is put on the library shelves in order. Then if somebody comes in, takes a book to look at and then shoves it back in the wrong place, it's not too difficult for the librarian to put it back in sequence.'

'So someone has to tidy up the books every so often?' said Teddy.

'They certainly do. Usually it's me! Ah—no O'Keefe under Geography. Shall I try History?'

'Yes, please,' said Maureen, adding, 'I do hope you have the book in the library!'

'Nothing under History either. Could it be listed under any other subject?'

'Ancient monuments or churches?' suggested Teddy.

'I'll try but I doubt it ... Wait a minute, you're right! There's a J.P. O'Keefe listed under monuments: *Landmarks of Connaught and Ulster*. Would that be what you are looking for?'

'Possibly!' agreed Maureen. 'Can we take the book home, please? We're all members of the library in Swinford.'

'I'm afraid that isn't possible. That book is locked in the history room. If you want to look at it you'll have to read it here. It's not for circulation.'

'That's all right,' said Teddy. 'We've enough time.'

'I'll unlock the cabinet for you,' said the librarian. 'You'll have to leave your schoolbags at the desk.'

'Why?' asked Kevin.

'In case you pinch any of the rare books!' whispered Teddy.

'I'll just get some paper from my bag,' said Maureen importantly. 'I may want to take notes.'

They followed the librarian into a small room at one side of the library. On the door was a notice: LOCAL HISTORY DEPARTMENT — AUTHORISED ACCESS ONLY in bold print. Teddy screwed up his face at it — he must be an Authorised Access! He wondered if that had anything to do with being an author.

'Here you are,' said the librarian. 'I'm going to shut the door. If you take any books from the cabinet, leave them down on the table when you have finished and I'll put them away myself. Oh — and don't touch any of the machines!'

Teddy looked longingly at the photocopier by the window but Maureen said firmly, 'We'll be very careful. Thanks very much.'

She scanned the shelves and soon found what she was looking for.

'Would you believe, there are four volumes? And they're huge! Boys, take one each!' She handed down two copies and took a third for herself. Kevin looked at the front cover of his.

'Volume 4, East Coast Counties. Shall I change it?'

'Yes, take this one. East Coast is a bit far away.'

For a while, the silence was disturbed only by the turning of pages. The books were the old-fashioned kind, printed on thick paper, with jagged edges where the pages had been originally joined and later roughly separated. This made turning the leaves a slow business as it was all too easy to miss a page. There were occasional sepia water-colours and black-and-white line drawings too, protected by inserts of transparent paper, and Maureen

32

cautioned the boys to be gentle as it would be very easy to tear them.

'I think I have something,' announced Teddy finally. 'This chapter is all about towers in Mayo and Donegal. Shall I read it through?'

'Have a quick look first to see if there are any diagrams,' said Maureen. 'We haven't time to read everything.'

Teddy thumbed through the chapter.

'There's a picture here of the round tower at Meelick,' he said. 'Exactly the same as it is today! It's amazing!'

'Keep going,' protested Kevin.

'Nothing ... nothing ... wait, here it is! Come here, it's the map!'

Kevin and Maureen leapt to their feet in excitement and came running round the table.

'There!' said Teddy. 'It's the same map! Compare it with my copy.'

He spread his photocopy beside the open page and there was no doubt at all — they were identical. Somebody had obviously made a rough copy from the printed map at some time, and added the compass reference and the author's name and date. But before it had been photocopied, the edge of the rough copy must have been torn — and several words, vital for the interpretation of the map, had been omitted.

'Look at the front of the book a moment, Teddy,' said Maureen. 'See when it was actually published.'

Teddy leafed back to the title page. 'London, 1879,' he read.

'There you are!' exclaimed Maureen. '*Our* copy was made in 1883! And just look what is printed on the bottom of the page, under the map!'

Legends exist that several other round towers, long since destroyed by time and the elements, were constructed on the Mayo plains. Some of these have vanished without trace, but antiquarians agree that the future may yield the remains of many others now forgotten.

The above map was reputedly sketched by a priest in the days of the struggles between Cathal of the Red Hand and Cathal Carrach, after he had fled from the burning monastery at Meelick with the "Druid gold" which had been stored there for safety. This map, thought to be of another round tower and monastery nearby, was reputed to show the ultimate resting place of this "gold". No proof that it ever existed has ever been found, and the location of this new round tower and monastery remains a mystery to this day. The only reference to the new location is the word "flavus" or "flavius" written beneath the word "flumen". This could be interpreted as referring to a personal name (Flavius was a prominent name in ancient Rome, being the family name of three emperors) and could be an indication that the "gold" consisted, in fact, of Roman coins struck during the reign of one of the Flavian emperors. The other possibility — that the word "flavus" (yellow) refers to one of the enemies of Cathal Rua — is, in the author's opinion, unlikely.

The map is located in the Parish Register in Foxford and is reproduced here by the kind permission of the Parish Priest.

'Well!' said Teddy. 'There you are! So it IS a treasure map, but not of Meelick. The treasure CAME from Meelick — our grumpy friend must have known that much — but it was taken from somewhere else.'

'Yellow!' repeated Kevin. 'Yellow ... yellow ... yellow! Sounds familiar...'

'... because we were talking about going to see Uncle Ed just before we came in here,' cut in Teddy. 'We were wondering if there was any fishing in the Yellow River down by his farm.'

'Yellow River!' said Maureen excitedly. 'Yellow isn't a name on a coin or a follower of Cathal Carrach. The new treasure location is on the Yellow River!'

'Which is miles long!' Teddy said immediately. 'So we go and dig the banks up on both sides! We'd need a couple of bulldozers.'

'No we wouldn't. What we need is a map of the river course. You wait here — and don't touch anything!'

She went out to the reception desk once more and waited until another man was seen to. Then she smiled at the librarian.

'We've found what we wanted — and now we need to look at one of the ordnance survey maps. Can we?'

'Oh, yes. Which one do you want?'

'The course of the Yellow River. Do you have that one?'

'We have them all. You wait in the history room and I'll bring them up to you.'

Maureen went back to the boys. Kevin had carefully written the missing details from the original map on to his copy, while Teddy admired the photocopy machine.

'Teddy!' cautioned Maureen. 'I hope you didn't touch

35

it? We don't want to be thrown out of here.'

'Don't be such an old hen! What do you take me for? I was just figuring out how it works. Mighty clever stuff.'

'Here you are!' announced the librarian, as she came into the room, staggering under the weight of the largest volume the children had ever seen. Behind her came a second girl with a second volume.

'We weren't sure which one of these two it was in, so we brought both,' explained the first librarian. She released her burden and it spread out, covering half of the table. 'That's heavy!'

Her companion, puffing, let her book slide down on top of the first. 'Be very careful with those now,' she cautioned. 'They are extremely valuable and very delicate. Would you like me to find the page for you?'

'You can stay and help them if you like, Helen,' said the first librarian. 'I'll get back to the desk.'

'Thanks,' agreed Maureen. 'It might be as well. Those pages are so big it would be very easy to break them.'

Helen opened one of the volumes and showed the children a large sectioned map of Mayo.

'Do you see how it works? Each section is numbered, and then you look up the map number you want.'

Maureen had found Callow Lake. 'The river is not far from there. That's the number we want.'

'I'll check it for you. Right — it's in this volume. I'll just turn the pages for you.'

The children watched amazed as the book unfolded before them. Turning the huge pages took some skill and Maureen was glad that Helen had offered to help. She would not like to have been blamed for tearing anything, and some of the sheets already showed a lot of wear. One

36

or two had come right out of the binding and had been put back out of order, but Helen replaced these as she went along.

'Here you are. Is this the one?'

'Thanks a lot. That's it. Oh, we've finished with those other books now. The other librarian told us to let her know, so she could put them away again.'

Helen picked up the three books.

'Well, that's a coincidence. You're the second person in a week to have these books down. I got them out myself only last week for a man who was doing some research. He isn't your teacher, is he? I mean, are you all working on a project for school?'

'Kevin is,' Teddy said quickly. 'But that man wasn't his teacher. Kevin's teacher is a woman.'

'What did the man look like?' asked Maureen. 'Quite fat with glasses?'

'Not at all. This fellow was very tall and thin and he hadn't shaved for at least two days. I remember wondering if it was safe to let him into the history room at all, he looked so fierce, but he was very polite and seemed to know what he was talking about. I expect he was one of these absent-minded professors. You know, the sort who forgets to have a shave and puts sugar on his dinner instead of salt.'

'Did he look at these survey maps as well?' Teddy wanted to know.

'There wasn't time. It was near closing-time when he came in. I suppose he'll be back one of the days to finish what he was doing. It would be nice if he came back while you children are here. That would save me having to get those heavy books out twice!'

'Yes, that would be just marvellous,' agreed Maureen, looking knowingly at Teddy.

'Well, I'll leave you to it for a few minutes. Call out if you need any more help. I'll be just outside.'

'Thanks very much,' said Teddy. Then, as she left the room, he stared at the other two. '*Another* man? Do you think there could be two people investigating the map now?'

'It sure looks like it,' Kevin answered. 'Quick, let's get our job done here and go. I don't want to meet any skinny men who don't shave.'

'Neither do I,' added Maureen. 'Now, everybody pay attention. Here's the Yellow River, and here's where it starts.'

'It runs right past Uncle Ed's place,' supplied Kevin.

'True. And this survey map was made in 1838 — look, it's printed on it — so anything in O'Keefe's books must be here too.'

'Don't forget that O'Keefe's map was a reproduction of a map made hundreds of years ago,' said Maureen. 'Even though the book was published long after the survey maps, the actual monk's map is much older.'

'So the tower might not be shown here.'

'But it is!' exclaimed Teddy. 'Look! Right on the river bank! Printed in that old-fashioned writing they use in church sometimes. "Round Tower" and a circle with a dot inside. That's it! That's the round tower!'

'Can we photocopy this page?' asked Kevin.

'I'll ask,' said Maureen. She went dashing out to the desk once more, where Helen was sorting out a pile of returned books.

'Can we make a photocopy of one of the survey maps?'

38

'I'm sorry,' answered Helen, 'it isn't permitted. There's a big notice on the binding cover. The volumes are far too heavy to lift on to the tray of the photocopier. They would break under their own weight. You can always make a sketch of the original, of course.'

'We aren't allowed to photocopy it,' explained Maureen on her return, 'and we have to leave soon anyway if we want that ride back home with Bob.'

Teddy looked at his own map again. 'The river has a little stream joining it just here, just like the two squiggles joining in the sketch map. That's simple enough to remember. And there are a couple of other things marked in, which should make it even easier to find. There are stepping-stones here, to the left of the tower, and some ruins on the other side of the river. We can compare them with Dad's small maps when we get home today, and then ask Maeve on Saturday when we visit Uncle Ed. It must be quite near their place.'

'That's the lot, so,' said Kevin. 'Let's get out of here before anyone else arrives to look for towers!'

That night, back at Rinn Mor, the children pored over one of their father's maps. A keen amateur historian and topographer, he kept several ordnance survey maps in his office, along with the invoices and orders for his carpentry business. Liam had joined the three McDonagh children and had been brought up to date with their findings in the library that afternoon. Now he was eager to see for himself the round tower marked on the banks of the Yellow River. But none of them could find it.

'I'm sure it was here,' said Teddy disappointed. 'Look, the stepping-stones are marked in, just the same as on

the map in Castlebar. The round tower was about a centi-
metre to the left of them.'

'Are you sure it's the same map?' asked Liam. 'I
wonder if the two maps were drawn by different people?'

'That's the point,' said Maureen. 'This map is dated
1915.'

'Surveyed 1896, revised 1915,' corrected Teddy. 'It
says so in the corner.'

'There you are then,' said Liam. 'Two different people
did the maps. Didn't you say the Castlebar maps were
done in 1835?'

'1838,' said Maureen. 'That's it then! The round tower
was no longer there when the second map was made.'

'The river is different on this map, too,' put in Teddy.
'I'm sure of it. The stepping-stones were on a straight bit
on the other map. Now they are on a bend.'

'Could be different stepping-stones,' said Kevin. 'The
old ones were washed away and they put new ones there.'

'No, it's more than that,' said Teddy. 'Get the photocopied map from my coat pocket, Kev. Let's have a look
at that. See?..' as he flattened out the photocopy of the
survey map, '... the river is not the same at all. This old
copy was exactly the same as the library map today, and
now there are squiggles all over the place on Dad's ver-
sion. Someone must have changed the river bed.'

'Reclaiming?' suggested Kevin.

'In those days? Unlikely!'

'But the river must have somehow changed course,'
said Maureen. 'We'll just have to be patient until we see
Uncle Ed. He's bound to know the answer.'

4   The Mill

'Hey, you're early!' yelled their cousin Maeve McGrath, as their car swerved and bumped its way down the little lane which led to her farm. She was perched on top of a huge boulder, her feet bare and her face smeared with blackberry juice.

'We didn't expect you before dinner. You'll have to make do with blackberries!'

Teddy stuck his head out of the open car window. 'Your mum invited us for dinner, so there! And I'm starving!'

'That's nothing new!' called back Maeve, leaping down nimbly from her perch and racing up the lane after the car. Her long legs, clad in an old pair of shorts, flashed in and out of the brambles and nettles but she emerged without injury, her freckled face beaming at them. 'Scratched your car again, Uncle Con!'

'I wonder why your father doesn't clip back some of those runners!' agreed her uncle. 'Every time I drive down this lane I have to get the car resprayed.'

'Doesn't bother us!' responded Maeve cheerfully. 'Our car is so old you wouldn't notice another scratch or two! Come on in, the cat's had kittens and they're in a box in the kitchen.'

The three children tumbled out of the car and ran up the cobbled farmyard to the house, trying to catch up with their cousin. Maeve had already disappeared inside, however, and they could hear her asking her mother when dinner would be ready. As they reached the door, Maeve's mother, Sile, came out to meet them, a cloth in her hands.

'I see you've all arrived! Dinner won't be for a while yet. Maeve, take them to see the goats. I'll call you when I want you.'

'Tassie had her kids,' explained Maeve. 'One boy and one girl. They are three days old, and we have them right by the house. Come on.'

She led the way and the cousins followed her, eager to see the babies. Tassie, a small Saanen with a wispy beard, was tethered to the wall beside the house. Near her the two kids slept, their little bellies as tight as two drums.

'All in noddy-land!' laughed Teddy. 'Let's go down to the river. We want to look at the river course?'

'Whatever for?' asked Maeve. 'That sounds like school work!'

'We'll explain on the way,' said Teddy. 'I have a map here and we want to go down and compare it with the river in real life.'

'If you insist ... but it sounds daft to me. The river goes on for miles.'

They left the farm buildings and began to climb slowly up the little track which wound its way through the fields. This was really rough mountain country now, and no farm machinery ever penetrated it deeply. Hills and valleys alike were carpeted in a thick sprinkling of rocks, many of them several feet high, and so far the land had resisted all efforts to reclaim it. This was the land of the goat and the blackface sheep and, of course, Uncle Ed's bees, who occupied a site half-way up the mountain at this time of year while the heather was in bloom.

Untamed though the landscape might appear, it was magic for a child. Instead of the orderly fields and tidy stone walls of the Rinn Mor farms, a fairyland sprawl of hillocks, hollows, jumbles of stone, thick patches of hazel and jungles of sycamore, ash and sloe provided a fantasy land for hide-and-seek, cops-and-robbers, and any other number of exciting games.

After they had crossed a stile to a neighbouring farm and skirted three fields, Maeve stopped.

'If you want to see the river spread out, we should climb to the top of this field. It's the highest point on this side of the valley and you can see for miles.'

'Lead on!' Teddy waved his map. 'We'll compare it with this.'

Maeve, in her bare feet, raced to the top of the hill like a hare. The other three, handicapped by shoes, made their way up more sedately. While Teddy unfolded his map and spread it out for them all to see, Maureen told Maeve about the man at Meelick and how they had checked up on the map he had dropped by looking in the old books and maps in the library.

'And you think there's an old tower on our river? That's exciting! But I don't know of anything like that. There's no tower certainly, and no buildings either — unless you count the old mill house, of course.'

'What old mill?' chorused Teddy and Maureen.

'The old mill on the river, silly. Didn't I ever take you there? It's not on our land, of course, but it's okay to go and look. The walls are sound — Dad had a good look at them in case I brought them down on top of me! You know, some old buildings can be dangerous. But he's given me the go-ahead to play down there.'

43

'Look at the river down there,' said Maureen. 'It IS a bit like the map. Look, there is a fork.'

'That's a tributary,' explained Maeve. 'That starts off as a spring a few kilometres up the fields, and joins in here with the main river. That's where the mill is, right at the join.'

'Shall we go and have a look?' asked Kevin. 'I'd love to see. Does anyone live there?'

'Not any more. A hundred years ago people used to bring their meal here to be ground into flour. There were at least ten buildings, and our lane would have been the main way in. It's all deserted now but the mill-wheel is still standing.'

'I think we should have a quick look,' decided Teddy, 'then go back for dinner. If we think it's worth investigating we could come back later.'

Just at that moment, however, Sile's voice came clearly across the fields, 'Children! Come and get it!'

'I suppose we'd better go,' said Maureen reluctantly. 'We'll gobble up double-quick and get back here as soon as we can.'

'I'm going to roll down the hill,' decided Kevin, and with one kick he had gone, rolling over and over until he bounced off a hawthorn tree at the level of the lane below and sat up with a loud 'Ouch!'

'Ready — set — go!' shouted Maeve, and the other three went down after him, Teddy holding the map screwed up tightly in his hand. Once at the bottom, they went racing back down the lane to the house. It was not far but the lane was winding and they were out of breath before the last corner was reached.

Inside the kitchen it was cool and dark, even though

there was a fire blazing on the hearth. Sile took a big pot from a hook and lifted it on to the tripod which stood waiting in the middle of the table. 'Hope you're all ready for stew!'

'Yum!' sniffed Teddy. 'You bet!'

She ladled out platefuls of the steaming stew, and then put a dish of potatoes on the table for everyone to help themselves. Before they had finished their first helpings, she served a second, so that even Teddy groaned, 'Help! I'll never eat all this!'

'There's cake to follow,' pointed out Sile, 'so you'd better leave room for that!'

'It's my birthday,' said Maeve smugly. 'I'm eleven today. Bet you didn't know.'

'We'll all have to sing,' announced Uncle Ed, and he began in a deep bass voice which made the children dissolve in fits of giggles... 'Happy birthday to you - ou - ou...'

As soon as the singing and cake eating was over the children excused themselves. Sile shooed them out of the kitchen, saying that as it was Maeve's birthday she would do the washing-up herself, and a few minutes later they were once more on their way to the far fields. This time they did not go up the hill but followed the lane until they came to the old mill, a cluster of stone buildings, some tumbledown and some almost intact, except for the roofs, of which only an occasional rafter remained.

'A hundred years ago this was a really important place,' explained Maeve. 'That building over there was the mill house. The old millstone is still there ...those bits of wood are all that is left of the mill-wheel.'

'Look at that stone!' exclaimed Teddy. 'It must have

taken a giant to move that. It's huge!'

> *I'm the king of the castle,*
> *And you're the dirty rascal!*

chanted Kevin, leaping on top of the stone.

'*I'm the king of the castle..* '

'You'll be some king if that stone tips!' declared Maureen. 'It's only balanced on its side.'

'Oh, it's always been like that,' Maeve said. 'I think it grew there!'

'Isn't it queer ... building the mill here?' asked Teddy. 'Wouldn't you think they would have built it on the edge of the river?'

'They did,' explained Maeve. 'Can't you see those rushes? The mill house was built over the river originally, where the swampy bit of ground is. The water ran right through the mill race and turned the wheel.'

'Of course — and then the river changed its course!' shouted Maureen. 'The river moved for some reason, and then they abandoned the mill.'

'Let's have another look at the old map,' said Teddy. 'I've got a feeling that we've solved the problem!'

He flattened the map out on the grass beside the mill-stone. Kevin jumped down and crouched beside him.

'Look,' said Teddy, 'here's the river, and here's the little tributary running in. See, Maeve? Well, this was the *old* river course. Now it's just the opposite, the same as Dad's modern map. The tributary is the river now and the original river has dried up to a swamp.'

'If that's true,' said Maureen, 'the round tower could be under the river.'

'According to the map,' said Teddy, 'there was either a

tunnel under or a bridge over the original river, running northwards from the square building to the round one.'

'Oh, most likely a tunnel,' decided Maureen. 'You know, like they used to have linking forts in the old days. Dan Moore has a fort on his land with a big souterrain, and it turns into a tunnel that leads right under the fields to Murtagh's fort. Or it did, until the sheep broke the walls in.'

'If there was a tunnel,' said Maeve, 'it could still be here! Where do you suppose it started?'

'Look at these squares on the old map,' answered Maureen. 'These must be the outlines of the original buildings. Let's see how they match up with what's here now.'

'Here's a pencil,' offered Teddy, pulling out his usual collection of junk from his pocket. 'Let's make a drawing of the modern site.'

'I'll do it,' and Maeve took the pencil from him, filling in the outlines of the tumbledown walls with a few quick strokes. 'And this is where the river goes.'

'It *is* the same place!' exclaimed Teddy. 'There are a couple of extra buildings now, but the group in the middle is exactly the same. Look, that long thin building is the old house, and the square one is the mill house.'

'Perhaps the little sheds were monks' cells in the old days,' said Maureen, '... if this really was a monastery.'

'Why a monastery?' asked Maeve.

'Because we're looking for a round tower that somehow has disappeared.'

'And there were always monasteries next to round towers, weren't there?' asked Kevin. 'So the mill house might have been a monastery once.'

'Unless it was always a mill,' answered Maeve. 'The miller may have sheltered the priest when he escaped from Meelick with the map and treasure.'

'Don't you remember the first survey map in Castlebar?' asked Maureen. 'There were ruins marked on it. Could the mill have been built on the site of the ruins?'

'Does it matter?' asked Kevin. 'In either case the treasure must still be under the round tower, and that's what Grumpy is looking for.'

'True ... but first we have to decide whether we have the right place here,' said Teddy. 'This river isn't exactly the same as our map. It matches Dad's new survey maps, but not ours.'

'But we've agreed that the river changed course,' said Kevin. 'This *has* to be the right place. All we have to do now is figure out how to find the round room.'

'Where do you suppose the tunnel begins?' asked Teddy. 'In the old dwelling house or in the mill house?'

'In the mill house, according to the map,' said Maureen. 'We'll try that first anyway.'

'Those old houses didn't have cellars,' said Maeve. 'Anyway, even if there was one once, it would be flooded now. The river would long ago have seeped in.'

'Maybe not,' said Maureen. 'The mill house is on a little rise, higher than the other buildings. Let's have a look.'

They pushed their way past the tangle of elder and hawthorn which had overgrown the walls. The doorway was still surmounted by its stone lintel, but this appeared to be quite solidly supported. Maureen recoiled as a robin, startled by all the activity, fluttered out of the elder, narrowly missing her face in its haste.

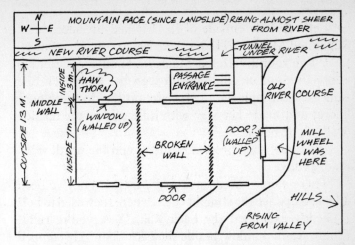

Inside the entrance, the entire flagged floor was a mass
of seedling trees which had sprung up over the years. The
roof was now formed of intertwined elder branches, and
even though the sunlight filtered through the greenery
and the day was warm, the children felt cold.

'If there's anything under any of these flags,' said
Maureen, 'we're going to have to throw a bomb in. This
lot hasn't been disturbed for hundreds of years, I'm sure.'

There were three rooms in the mill house, which was
built after the traditional western pattern — three rooms
in a straight line, with the gable walls facing east and west.
One door faced south; a second, which had originally
been opposite the south door, had been blocked up with
large rocks. Time had woven a jungle of honeysuckle
around them and they were firmly anchored in position.

'Nothing in here,' said Teddy.

'What about the fireplaces?' asked Maureen.

'No ... the floor is earth there. No way anything could
be underneath.'

'Let's try the outside of the blocked-up door then,' suggested Maeve. 'Perhaps there was a porch there once.'

'I'll go round,' offered Maureen. 'You stay here. No sense in all of us climbing through the lot twice!' She squeezed through the thicket around the doorway once more, and made her way with difficulty to the outside wall of the house.

'It's funny there were no windows on the north side,' said Teddy.

'There were, once,' answered Maeve. 'They've been blocked up. See the straight edges where they used to be?'

Teddy examined the back wall. 'Yes, you're right. There was a window beside the back door.' He stepped through the tumbledown partition into the west room. 'The back window in this room is blocked up too.'

'And in this one,' added Kevin from the small east room. 'Every single window and door on the back of the house has been well blocked up. I can't even see daylight through.'

The sound of branches cracking and leaves rustling made them turn to the entrance. Maureen burst in, her hair full of twigs and her face red with exertion.

'What's the matter with you lot? I've been on the river bank, on the other side of that wall, shouting my head off, and nobody answered.'

'We've been here all the time,' said Maeve. 'We heard nothing.'

'I've been yelling at the top of my voice,' repeated Maureen. 'I was only just on the other side of the back wall.'

'In that case,' observed Teddy curiously, 'just how thick is that wall?'

5 The Secret Room

The children looked at one another in excitement.

'Are you thinking what I'm thinking?' asked Teddy.

'There's only one explanation,' agreed Maureen.

Maeve and Kevin looked bewildered.

'What's the big secret?' asked Kevin.

'It's obvious,' said Maureen. 'There has to be some kind of space in there — a hidden room or passage. That would explain why you couldn't hear me when I shouted.'

'A secret passage!' repeated Kevin with glee. 'Lovely! How do we get in?'

'There must be a secret panel,' decided Teddy.

'In the stone?' mocked Maeve. 'You're brilliant!'

'It has to be something more basic. A stone on a pivot could be what we want,' said Maureen.

'Isn't it possible that the room was just walled up?' put in Kevin quietly. 'Perhaps we have to pull part of the wall down to get in there.'

'That's more like it!' agreed Teddy heartily. 'For once you've come up with something sensible! Everyone look for a bit of wall that's too regular to be true.'

'There's the door shape, of course,' said Maeve. 'That's regular. My guess is, they simply blocked up the door and the windows and left it at that.'

'If there were windows they must have been on an outside wall at one time,' said Maureen.

'How are we going to move all those stones?' asked

Kevin. 'Some of them are real boulders! Giants must have rolled them into place.'

'Silly us!' exclaimed Teddy. 'We don't need to move any at all. There isn't any roof. All we have to do is climb over the top! We just have to move some of those branches at the top and then we can climb in.'

'We need a pair of hedge-clippers,' said Maeve. 'Dad has some. I'll go back to the house and get them, while you have a scout around here.'

Maureen paced the length of the wall, counting. 'The inside wall measurement is seven metres. I'm going to pace the outside now.'

Teddy joined her. 'Me too. I'm the maths wizard.'

'It doesn't take a genius to measure this!' was Maureen's answer. 'I've counted nine metres already and there must be another three at least where I can't get in through the trees. Even allowing for the thickness of the wall that still leaves three or four metres to spare.'

'I think I've worked it out,' said Kevin, coming to meet them. 'Before there was a mill here it was a monastery. The room was a secret hiding-place for valuables.'

'No,' answered Teddy, shaking his head. 'The room must have been made later, after the windows were walled up. Either that or the room was originally part of the mill and somebody wanted people to forget its existence.'

'I wish Liam had come!' sighed Kevin. 'He'd have some ideas.'

'I'm going to climb to the top of the wall here,' announced Teddy. 'I might be able to see something. Give me a lift up, Maureen. I can sit on the top here where it isn't too thorny.'

Maureen bent her knee against the wall and Teddy scrambled up, putting one foot on her knee and the other on to her cupped hand. She pushed upwards and he tumbled on to the top of the wall, scraping his knee on the stones.

'Ouch! That was a rough ride!'

'Can you see anything up there, Teddy?' called Kevin.

'Not much. The middle of the wall is a bit far away. I can just see in over the top. '

'Is there any roof left?' asked Maureen.

'None at all, but the whole thing is full of bushes. There's a big hawthorn tree right in the middle as far as I can see, so there won't be much room left for us.'

'Can you see up the hill? Is Maeve coming?'

'Yes, I see her. Hedge-clippers and a rope as well.'

'Hi!' shouted Maeve, catching a glimpse of him on top of the wall. 'See anything?'

'No! Hurry up with those clippers. I'm going to walk along to the middle wall.'

Teddy rose delicately and began to make his way along the top of the stone wall, dislodging a few small stones which came crashing down beside Kevin and Maureen.

'Be careful, Teddy!' yelled Kevin. 'You could come down with the stones.'

'It's quite safe,' said Teddy.

Just then an especially large stone began to rock and then suddenly gave way, bringing him down in a heap right in the middle of a blackberry bush.

'I'm not going to say I told you so!' stated Maureen.

'Lucky that bush was there to catch me. I feel like I've sat on a porcupine.'

'Why don't I go up?' suggested Kevin. 'I'm lighter

than Teddy, so it would be safer.'

'We'll lift you,' said Maeve. 'Have a look and see what it's like in there.'

Seconds later Kevin had been positioned on the middle wall and was looking down into the secret room.

'Can't see a thing,' he said. 'It's quite dark with all the undergrowth and stuff. You'll have to come up and look for yourselves.'

'What's the wall like?' asked Maeve. 'Can we all get up there at once?'

'There's a big flat stone up here. I must be over one of the windows. It seems quite firm.'

'You're on one of the lintels,' explained Teddy. 'Move over, I'm coming up.'

This time he was able to get a foothold in the old window and he made his way up to his brother without assistance. 'Throw up those clippers, Maeve. We can't get down inside until I've got rid of a few of these branches.'

Maeve handed them up and Teddy began clipping, throwing the discarded branches back down to the girls.

'I'm beginning to see now. That hawthorn tree is growing in the actual wall, would you believe it? It's not in the floor at all.'

'How long before we can come up?' demanded Maeve impatiently.

'Throw me the rope and I'll tie it on to the hawthorn. I can just reach the trunk.'

Maeve slung up one end and Teddy caught it deftly. 'Here, Kevin, grab my legs just in case I slip. I'll tie the rope, then you go down first.'

Kevin grasped the cuffs of Teddy's jeans while the

latter leaned forward. He managed a double-reef knot around the trunk of the tree and pulled it to test.

'It seems fast enough. Go now, Kev, and I'll take the slack.'

Kevin took hold of the knotted free end of the rope and began to descend the wall, kicking himself clear of the stones with his runners. Teddy guided the rope, gradually lessening his hold on it until Kevin was supported by the tree alone.

'I'm down,' he called. 'Come on, Teddy, there's a queer thing down here!'

'Coming,' said Teddy. 'You girls can follow me. The rope is okay. See you down there!'

With that Teddy swung himself out into the air and landed down beside Kevin.

'You're right! Look at that hole there. Do you think we can get in?'

The boys were looking at what appeared to be a rectangular opening in the ground, outlined with stones. A slab of slate partially covered it and was obviously intended to seal over the opening when in place.

'It looks like a fish-pond,' suggested Kevin. 'Can we pull that old stone out of the way and get rid of a few of those weeds?'

'Shall I bring the clippers?' called Maeve from the top of the wall.

'Yes, hand them down,' answered Teddy. 'Thanks. Come on down now yourself.'

He began to cut away some of the larger plants. Over the years grasses and small weeds had sprouted between the irregular flagstones of the floor, and the immense hawthorn which was growing from the base of one of the walls overshadowed the space where the roof had once been. Maureen, the last to descend, began to help him by pulling away the smaller clumps and the others joined in, eager to see what the opening would be. Finally all four tugged at the slate and with difficulty the four of them managed to slide it to one side. An army of woodlice scuttled for shelter and several fat slugs uncurled.

But the children were not looking at the slugs. They were staring in astonishment as they realized that this was no fish-pond — it was a stone staircase!

'Where do you think it leads?' asked Kevin. 'Let's see!'

'Not so quickly!' protested Maeve. 'It might be dangerous. We wouldn't be able to see our way.'

'Well, I'm going!' declared Teddy. 'It's only stone, not wood. It will be quite safe. I want to see where it goes!'

He edged his way past the undergrowth which still partly choked the entrance and began to feel his way down. The staircase descended steeply and there was nothing to hold on to but Teddy kept one hand on the roof which was only inches above his head and appeared to slope at the same angle as the staircase.

'I'm coming too!' said Maeve. 'How far are you?'

'I'm down about twelve steps,' said Teddy, 'and ... whoops!'

'What's wrong?' called Maureen. 'Are you all right?'

'I'm all right but I'm wet through! I slipped — and the staircase goes straight into a big puddle. It must have been some kind of well.'

'Are you soaked?' asked Kevin.

'Completely! I'll have to come out to dry off. We'd better leave any more exploring until we get a torch.'

'I bet that's the reason the room is sealed off,' decided

Maureen. 'The well was dangerous and they shut it off.'

'Why would they want a well when the river was so near?' asked Kevin. 'Wouldn't the river water have been good enough?'

'Could have been shallower in those days,' suggested Maeve. 'They might have thought it was too muddy.'

'Poor old me!' announced a dripping Teddy, emerging from the stairwell.

'Take off your shirt at least,' ordered Maureen. 'That will get some of you dry.'

Teddy stripped off his shirt as she suggested and bent to remove his runners and socks. A cupful of dirty water flowed out of each runner as he removed it.

'Yuk!' exclaimed Kevin. 'That stinks!'

'Stagnant,' agreed Teddy. 'If that ever was a well it sure isn't fit for drinking any more. And more fool me to put my shoes back on before dinner!'

'We'll go back to the house,' said Maeve. 'I can lend Teddy something to wear and that will be a perfect excuse for you to come back next week-end! Next time we'll have a torch ready and we'll all go in. In the meantime I'll come over here after school each day and cut some more of the undergrowth away.'

'Brilliant,' said Kevin. 'We'll get Liam to come too.'

'Who's Liam?' Maeve wanted to know.

'A friend of ours from the next village,' said Maureen. 'He helped us get the cross back last July.'

'Yes, you told me about that.'

They shinned up the rope again and down into the part of the house they had first explored. Teddy threw his wet clothes over first, then came up after them.

'I can hear someone calling us,' announced Kevin.

'Listen, it's Auntie Sile.'

'I couldn't eat another thing,' declared Maureen. 'I hope she isn't going to feed us again.'

They climbed the stile once more and crossed the McGrath lands back to the house. The adults were sitting outside on the stone seat by the door, sipping mugs of tea.

'And what have you been doing, Teddy?' enquired Con sternly. 'Falling in the river at your age?'

Teddy did not answer, just shrugged.

'Shall I lend him some clothes?' asked Maeve.

'Yes, you'd better. Go with her, Teddy; she'll get you something dry.'

'And don't drip all over the clean floor,' added his father.

'I've drip-dried already,' answered Teddy.

'He's ready for the spin cycle!' added Maureen.

Teddy followed Maeve into the house and accepted the clean clothes. 'Here's a plastic bag,' she offered. 'Put your wet stuff in here and don't be smelling my room out.'

'Thanks,' answered Teddy. 'Go and make the arrangements about next week now, while they think it's a good idea.'

Maeve left him to change and went out to her parents and uncle. 'I've lent Teddy my grey tracksuit,' she informed them. 'I have to have it back for our gymnastics inter-club night next Sunday. Can you come out next Saturday for the day and return it?'

'Good idea!' agreed Kevin quickly. 'Is that okay, Dad?'

'I guess so,' said Con. 'I've a few daffodil bulbs for you, Ed, and the weather is ideal for putting them in.'

Maureen grinned at Maeve in delight. This was

working out very nicely. For once Teddy had engineered one of his mishaps to their advantage!

'Is it all right if one of our friends comes as well?' asked Kevin. 'We had sort of planned to spend the day together.'

'Fine,' said Ed, winking at his brother-in-law. 'Is he any good at planting daffodils?'

'Oh, fantastic!' declared Maureen. 'No sweat!'

'Wear a wetsuit next time, Teddy,' advised Ed, 'if you plan to go falling in any more rivers. It's a good thing the river changed course and flattened out a bit, or you might have been in real trouble.'

They all turned to look at the doorway, and burst out laughing at the sight of the bold adventurer, for Maeve's tracksuit was too short and Teddy's bare feet, topped by a mud-stained expanse of bare ankle, stuck out prominently.

But Maureen did not join in. 'What's that about the river changing, Uncle Ed?' she asked quickly.

'There isn't much to tell, really. The river used to run straight past the field at the end of the house, and right down the valley near the mountain.'

'There were several mills on the river then,' added Sile. 'In fact there is the ruin of one of them quite close to our fields.'

'Yes, we've seen it,' said Kevin eagerly. 'Maeve told us it was still working a hundred years ago.'

'Quite right. Then there was a landslide and the river was diverted away from the buildings. This was about the time that a lot of people were leaving the west and going abroad, so the mill was simply abandoned. A family moved in at one time and tried to start a little farm, but it

59

was too isolated and they moved out as well,' Ed grinned at the children. 'If you think our place is old-fashioned, you can imagine what it was like down there in winter!'

'Was there a round tower around here one time?' asked Teddy.

'Funny you should ask that,' replied Ed. 'I haven't thought about that since I was a boy. Your mother and I often hunted for the Lost Tower, as we used to call it, but in the end we decided it was only a legend.'

'Tell us, please!' begged Kevin.'

'The story was that there was a tower on the river bank once. That was long before the landslide, when there would have been flat land on both sides. It was supposed to be on the north bank.'

'There *is* a round tower shown on the old maps,' said Maureen. 'It's on the one done in 1838, but it's missing from the modern ones.'

'There you are then,' said Ed. 'It must have been buried in the landslide.'

'I wonder why nobody has ever tried to excavate it?' said Maureen.

'I don't suppose anyone ever took it seriously,' answered Sile. 'Some of those landmarks on the old maps would have been in ruins even when the maps were drawn up. Besides, you couldn't start digging the whole mountainside. There might be another landslide!'

'We could take a picnic down the river next week-end and figure it out,' said Maeve.

The children settled themselves reluctantly. For once, Teddy was not hungry. He could not wait to get back home and bring Liam up to date with the day's findings. When he was safely back in his own jeans, of course!

60

6 Caught!

That week had to be the longest in the children's lives!
School seemed interminable, and even the fact that
Kevin was praised for his detailed drawing of the Meelick
round tower, and had the honour of seeing it in pride of
place on the classroom notice-board, did not compensate.
Liam had been told the story over and over again, and
they had spent hours each evening after school poring
over the map, trying to determine what the staircase
could be and where it could lead to.

The arguments went on all week, but they had still
come to no conclusion when Friday night arrived at last.
That night Liam did not come to visit as he wanted to get
his chores finished as far as possible so he would be free to
come with them the next day. They planned an early start
and Liam was to be collected on the way.

Eileen McDonagh decided to come too, much to the
children's delight. That meant a long stay. If their father
was on his own, he was always in a hurry to get back to
Rinn Mor, but their mother was quite happy to stay and
chat the night away! The daffodil bulbs were safely
packed in the boot, along with some new crop apples from
Dan Moore's trees for their picnic and some home-made
bread, Eileen's speciality.

Maeve was waiting, perched on her rock again, waving
furiously as their car rounded the last bend and shouting
to them long before they had a hope of making out what
she was saying.

'I bet she's after her tracksuit!' laughed Maureen.

Con drew to a halt beside the house and the four children jumped out, eager to be started on their way. Maeve danced around them, full of excitement.

'We've got a visitor! ... Are you Liam? Hullo, Liam, I'm Maeve ... The visitor is in the kitchen. He's a Professor! Did you bring my tracksuit back, Teddy?'

Teddy flung open the boot.'Here's your tracksuit! And the grub, and the daffodil bulbs.'

'I've made sandwiches,' said Maeve. 'Ooh, good, you've got some of Auntie Eileen's bread. Never mind, we'll have that too! Come on in the kitchen and we'll pack it all in one bag.'

The children followed her into the house, and stopped in amazement when they saw who the visitor was. Grumpy from Meelick Tower! Obviously he was just as taken aback to see them.

'This is Professor Quinn,' announced Aunt Sile. 'My two nephews and their friend, and my niece Maureen.'

'Liam O'Connor,' supplied Liam. 'Pleased to meet you, Mrs. McGrath — and you, Professor Quinn,' he added politely.

The Professor frowned. Then he said to Sile, 'I didn't realize all these children would be around. I hope they will not bother me? I won't be very long.'

'Of course not.' Sile turned to the children. 'Professor Quinn is an archaeologist, from Dublin. He's going to take some photos of the old mill. He thinks it might have some historical importance, especially as it was there before the landslide in 1890.'

Professor Quinn tucked a folded paper into his pocket, but not before Teddy had caught a glimpse of the corner.

'Well, I'll be off, Ma'am. Thank you for giving me permission to work on your farm.'

'Oh, it's not our land,' answered Sile. 'Our land goes as far as the stile, then it's Farrelly's. But there's no dwelling house there so you wouldn't find anyone to ask. As long as you shut all the gates there's no problem.'

'I will that. Thank you.' He looked at the children, his eyes narrowing. 'I expect to be able to work undisturbed. I would appreciate that.' He nodded to Sile and marched out, his heels clicking on the cobbles.

'Oh dear!' exclaimed Sile. 'I should have warned him to wear boots. He won't get too near the river in those things!'

'City-slicker!' agreed Ed, who had just come in with his sister and brother-in-law. 'Who was that?'

'A Professor Quinn,' answered Sile. 'He is doing research and came to ask permission to photograph the old mill.'

'Whatever for? It's the same as hundreds of others and much harder to get at.'

'Is it all right if we go?' put in Maeve impatiently. She had seen the looks exchanged by her three cousins and knew something must be up!

'Yes, you kids go. But you heard what he said. Stay away from the mill so he can work in peace!'

'That's a bit of a cheek,' grumbled Maeve. 'We were going to have our picnic there.'

'It's far too early to eat. Why don't you go up the mountain for a walk? You could take your sandwiches.'

'Yes, good idea,' said Maureen. 'Come on, Liam, help me put our stuff with Maeve's and we can take turns carrying the bags.'

Very soon everything was in two small rucksacks, in one of which Maeve had put a rope and a torch.

'Anyone got a watch?' called Con as they left.

'Me,' answered Teddy and Maeve simultaneously.

'Okay, get back here by five. That gives you time to climb at least two mountains!'

'Come ON!' urged Maeve, hurrying them round the corner of the sheds. 'Now, out with it! Who was that man?'

'That's was Grumpy!' said Liam. 'The same fellow that was sneaking around the tower at Meelick.'

'And,' put in Teddy, 'I saw what was in his pocket. It was a corner of the old ordnance survey map! He is right on the same trail as we are.'

'And not only that, if he's from Dublin then I'm a Kerryman!' shouted Liam. 'He knew I was a traveller when he saw us at the round tower. He must be a local man to know that.'

'Yes, you're right,' agreed Kevin. 'If he knew who you were, he had to be from Swinford or around that way.'

'He recognized all of us today, I'm sure of that,' said Maureen. 'We'll have to be extra careful to keep out of his way. I doubt that he's a professor at all, or why would he be telling lies about being from Dublin?'

'We'd better be on our guard,' agreed Teddy. 'Anyway we promised Auntie Sile to keep out of his way. Only problem is, I want to keep an eye on him.'

'We only promised we'd climb the hill,' pointed out Maeve. 'And we will. We'll just go the roundabout way to the mill. We can cross the river higher up and approach it from the opposite side. That way we can come quite close to him while he does his "research"!'

They set off up the hills in single file. If any of the grown-ups happened to be watching, they would have assumed that the children were beginning the ascent. Instead, they intended to double back once they had reached the first line of bushes and return to the riverside.

The mountainside track led up steeply, crossing a little log bridge which just cleared the torrent, then rising sharply amidst the rocks. Some of the boulders were as big as houses and the track went around them. Originally the way had been formed over the generations by the feet of thousands of sheep, and fresh droppings here and there showed that sheep had been that way not long before. Sure enough, as they reached one huge boulder they came across several ewes cropping at the tufts of rough purple moor grass and heather. They eyed the children inquisitively, then as Teddy mouthed "Boo!" they gave a little skip and melted away one after the other.

'Meanie!' said Maureen. 'They were tame. I could have petted one.'

'Don't you be so sure about that,' contradicted Maeve. 'When we come to round them up, it isn't the quickest job I know. We can be after them all day up in the hills, and they just stay out of reach, laughing at us.'

'Doesn't your dog help?' asked Kevin.

'He does all the work. Dad and I couldn't get them down at all without him.'

'There's a rabbit!' exclaimed Liam. Not ten metres in front of them was a half-grown brown rabbit, his ears pricking up as he watched them approaching.

'That fellow will be far tamer than the sheep,' observed Maeve. 'You can get amazingly close to them if you pretend you're not really interested. Look!' She dropped to her knees and began to crawl towards the rabbit. Instead of going at a steady rate, however, she moved forward two or three paces, stopped, moved again, stopped, then turned her head slightly towards the other children as if to indicate that she was not at all interested in the rabbit. All the time, however, she was watching him out of the corner of her eye. By now he could see her coming, but although he was alert and ready to run, he made no move until there was a bare metre separating them. Only then, as if to show he was weary of the game, did he wheel around delicately and hop away with a little flick of his hind legs.

'There you go!' she declared, scrambling back to her feet. 'Tame as any farm animal!'

'How far before we turn back?' inquired Liam.

'Just past this next rock. We can get right back to the river by sliding down the slope. The further you go along this bank, the steeper the drop gets. By the time you have reached the mill, it's far too steep to go down.'

Maeve sat down, gave herself a little push off, and went sliding down the slope at top speed.

'I'll get all dirty!' complained Maureen.

'Only dusty,' contradicted Teddy, following his cousin down. 'Come on, we'll leave you behind.'

Kevin and Liam followed in quick succession and finally, if reluctantly, Maureen followed. They had finished in thick scrub, but still the sheep track led on through. The animals had trodden and eaten their way into it over the years until there was a permanent passage through the vegetation. The children were able to file through without difficulty, one after the other, and quite soon Maeve, who was leading the way, turned back to caution them. 'We're getting near the mill now. Better keep quiet or Professor Grumpy might hear us!'

'Right you are,' replied Liam, who was second in line, and he turned to warn the others. They continued on, aware now of any twig or fallen leaf which threatened to rustle or crackle and thus betray them. Once or twice Maeve stopped and listened, only to trudge on again. After a few more minutes of tiptoeing and controlled breathing, she stood still and waved to them all to do likewise. Then she parted the branches of an alder which overhung the water and peered through. Liam, looking over her shoulder, could see that the mill was directly opposite, on the other side of the river, but there was no sign of Grumpy.

Maeve released the branches carefully and looked back at him.

'What now?' she asked. 'I can't see him.'

'Well, keep quiet anyway!' warned Liam. 'That doesn't mean he isn't there.'

'He won't hear us above the sound of the river if we just whisper,' said Maeve. Indeed the river was particularly noisy just here as it had to cross several rocks wedged in the riverbed, and there were little eddies and miniature waterfalls breaking up the main stream beside the mill. Water boatmen swirled around in their dizzy circles in the swampy shallows, and midges hung in little clouds above them.

'There he is!' hissed Kevin, and at once all five children froze. Grumpy had suddenly emerged from the old mill building and, like the children, he seemed to be counting the paces from one end of the building to the other.

'He is working out about the secret room!' whispered

Teddy in dismay. 'He'll find our rope next and climb in! We shouldn't have left it there last week-end.'

'We didn't,' whispered back Maeve. 'I came and got it and the clippers during the week. He won't be able to get in unless he has his own.'

Grumpy was writing in a notebook now, and as the children watched he turned on his heel and went back around the building.

'Look!' said Teddy. 'He's off up the hill. He must have given up until he can find a way in.'

'Let's go, quickly, before he comes back!' urged Kevin. 'Leave the picnic here and just bring the torch.'

'Hey — who has the torch?' asked Teddy. 'We all forgot it!'

'I didn't!' replied Maeve smugly. 'It's under the sand-wiches, and I brought the rope back as well. See, smarty?'

'Well done!' said Liam. 'Now, how do we get across the river?'

'By the stepping-stones, of course,' answered Maeve. 'Follow me and watch where I put my feet.' She stripped off her runners and socks and demonstrated. A few seconds later she was on the opposite shore, waving to them. Maureen unearthed the rope and torch and handed them to Liam. 'Here ... you're the tallest. If you fall in with them they are less likely to float away!'

'Thanks very much!' grinned Liam, and leapt across as deftly as Maeve had done.

'Here goes,' announced Kevin, and no one was more surprised than he was when he landed on the mill-house side with only his toes wet. Maureen and Teddy followed without mishap, and they all made their way around the blackberries to the outer door, treading carefully to avoid the thorns. This was no area for bare feet!

Teddy pointed out the section of the wall that they had cleared the last time, and he and Liam swarmed up and soon had the rope in position. One at a time they dropped down into the inner room, still regretting the missing footwear.

'Those are the steps,' said Teddy, pointing. 'It's slippery down there. I'm going to be more careful this time!'

Liam shone the torch into the opening, and the reflection off the brackish water cast an eerie green light on the stone walls.

'It's a staircase all right,' agreed Liam, stepping down into it. 'The question is, what did it lead to?'

'I still say it led to a cellar,' said Maeve. 'The mill was in use up to a hundred years ago, and the river would have still been flowing under the mill-house in those days.'

Liam made his way further into the stairwell, shining his torch up and down as he went.

'Whatever it was, it's been here a long time,' he asserted. 'These steps are well worn and the sides are smooth as though people rubbed against them.'

'What about the water?' asked Teddy.

'Rainwater. Or seepage from the river. Whatever it is, that is the most likely reason they walled up the room. It would be dangerous for cattle if they slipped and fell in.'

'Children too,' said Maeve. 'Daddy can remember a family living here when he was growing up. That was long after the mill closed down, of course. That big shed there was a thatched cottage once. They left when Daddy was about twelve.'

Liam stepped into the water. Feeling his way with his

toes, he descended gingerly. When the water reached the rim of his rolled-up jeans, he stepped back again.

'Whatever it leads to, it's deep. I can't get in any further without getting soaked, and the steps seem to go down a long way still. No wonder you got wet through, Teddy. There must be a great collection of moss and slimy things on these rocks.'

'Not to mention the nasties!' added Teddy. 'What do you want to bet this place is full of leeches?'

'Quiet!' ordered Maureen. 'I think I hear Grumpy! Quick, let's get out of here and back over to our own side of the river.'

She swung herself up to the top of the wall and shaded her eyes with one hand. 'Yes, he's coming! I can just see through the branches. There's someone with him and they have a ladder! He *has* guessed about this place. Follow me, hurry!'

She leapt down and within seconds Kevin and Maeve had joined her. Maeve tugged at the tell-tale rope and snatched it up as it coiled down at her feet. They scrambled into the cover of the blackberries behind one of the fallen internal walls, just in time to escape detection as the two men rounded the corner of the old house. Teddy and Liam had been cut off!

The two men did not look in the direction of the black-berry bushes at all, but made their way immediately to the back wall and stood the ladder against it.

'I told you we'd need something to climb up,' said Grumpy. 'Get up there and see what's on the other side.'

'It had better be worth my while,' snarled the second man. The children could see him plainly now, and Maureen nudged Kevin sharply.

'Look,' she whispered. 'The man who was at the library!'

Grumpy's companion certainly matched the description Helen had given them. Tall and extremely thin, he had a long bony face and a black stubble which had not seen a razor for at least two days.

Maureen held her breath as he ascended the ladder. Would he see the two boys?

'The steps are just as you said,' he asserted. 'I can see them from here. Now what?'

'Get down the other side, of course, then tip the ladder back over to me. Don't take all day about it or we'll have those interfering kids after us.'

'No worry about them. Their mother sent them off up the hill. I saw them starting out a while back.'

So Stubble had been spying on them! Maeve drew in an indignant breath but Maureen pinched her to be quiet. Bad enough if the boys were discovered, but at least the three of them on the outside had remained undetected.

'I'm down!' shouted Stubble. 'Throw the gear over.'

A rubber torch went sailing over the wall, followed by a field compass, a rope and a pickaxe, Maureen surmising that these items must have been hidden there for some time, as Grumpy and Stubble had not been carrying anything other than the ladder when they arrived.

Grumpy followed the pickaxe, and the children heard them stumbling through the undergrowth to the steps. In another minute they would see the boys at the bottom of the stairwell, and then what would happen? Kevin was rigid in the bush, oblivious of the thorns sticking into him everywhere, his eyes tight shut in the hope that by some miracle the men would not discover Liam and Teddy.

7 Into The Tunnel

When Teddy and Liam realized that they had no chance
of getting back across the wall before the men saw them,
they looked around frantically to see if there was any
hiding-place. The foliage of the old tree was thick, but not
dense enough to hide them completely, and the other
growth was too short to be useful. They crouched down
in the stairwell just as Stubble reached the top of the wall.
There was now no way they could get out without being
seen! Liam backed down into the water until it was up to
his knees.

'Get down, Teddy!' he hissed. 'It's our only chance.
When they come to look down, hold your breath and
hope they don't have a torch. Remember, it's quite dark
in here when you look down from above.'

Teddy waded down to Liam. It was bitterly cold but he
was in such a state of tension that he barely noticed it.
Liam was holding the torch but did not dare to turn it on.
Slowly he backed towards the wall. To his surprise, what
he had taken for a bare wall was an opening! Carefully he
took a step forward and found that the ground, too, had
levelled out. He had been standing on the bottom tread
and had not realized it.

'Quick, Teddy! Follow me!'

Teddy, amazed to see Liam disappearing, felt his way
forwards and joined him.

'We're safe! Unless they come after us, they will never
guess there's an opening here. Let's see how far it goes!'

Although Liam could not risk using the torch, the boys could see vaguely where they were going. A faint light reflected off the tunnel walls, and this was accentuated by a slight phosphorescence on the surface of the water.

'It's the tunnel in the map,' Teddy said softly.

'Looks as though we've found it, right enough.'

Liam moved on awkwardly, feeling his way one foot at a time. Teddy, anxious not to be left on his own, waded after him gently, trying not to splash and draw attention to themselves. The roof and floor rose gradually together and soon their feet were clear of the water.

Teddy estimated that they had travelled some ten metres when Liam suddenly stumbled and the boys realized that they had reached a second set of steps. This time the way led upwards, and soon they were on level ground again. There was no light at all here so they could not imagine where they could be, and they stood there for a moment, trying to make out their surroundings.

Teddy became aware of a strange booming noise in the tunnel and looked towards Liam in horror. Liam, a strange shadowy shape in the darkness, felt rather than saw his friend's terrified stare, and tapped his hand sharply to warn him to keep quiet. Then Teddy realized what the weird sound was. The men were talking, at the first set of steps, and their voices were echoing through the airspace in the tunnel, rebounding in the opening where the boys were sitting.

'This is the first staircase,' said one.

'Where does it lead to?'

'If my father was right, we follow it for twelve paces. That will bring us to the second set of steps, and they lead straight up into the tower.'

'You have to be kidding! Twelve paces and we'll be inside that mountain there.'

'Right! There was a landslide here a hundred years ago and the tower ruins were covered. The river changed course as well, and the tunnel filled up, level with the new water-table. It's all swamp here now, and of course the tower itself is rubble. We'll have to dig in from outside.'

'Why did your grandfather never come back to claim it himself?'

'My *great* grandfather. He died soon after the landslide and left the old map with his son — that was my grandfather — together with a couple of pages of notes. That map was out of date after the landslide, of course, but the new survey maps were made soon after and they show the modern river course. That's how I worked out where to look in the first place — by comparing the two. The old dolt never wrote down the location anywhere. No wonder it took me so long to find the place. I had been looking for a tower which was still standing, not one which had been in ruins so long it had been forgotten.'

'How come your father and grandfather never tried to find it?' The voice sounded suspicious.

'Grand-da went to England as a youngster and never bothered — I think he thought the whole thing was a bit of a hoax. Just before he died he gave the papers to my father, but *he* decided he was too old at that stage for treasure-hunting, so he passed them on to me. I've been trying to find the right place ever since.'

'I hope it *isn't* a hoax!' growled the second man. 'You'd better not be leading me on with your fine promises.'

'Would I be wasting my time if I wasn't sure? I checked out the story with the old records and it all fits.

The photocopies you made for me at the library confirm everything. You'll get your share, never fear. Now all we have to do is to find the correct place to dig. We're at the tunnel entrance here, and the tunnel ran north-north-east. So we take a compass bearing, pace out the ten metres and start digging.'

While this conversation had been taking place, Liam and Teddy were listening in dismay. They were inside the mountain then — perhaps inside the very ruins the men had been discussing! They strained their ears to hear more, but the mens' voices gradually became fainter and finally became quite inaudible. They stayed where they were, however. It would not do to move too soon in case the men had not gone far enough.

At the other side of the tumbledown building, Kevin had got so worried about Liam and Teddy that he had crept out of his bush and tiptoed over to the middle wall to listen. He, too, had overheard the men and was so busy trying not to miss a word that he was taken completely by surprise when a large hand suddenly took hold of his tee-shirt and lifted him off the ground.

'Might have known you kids couldn't stay away! Spying, are you?'

'Oh, no, Professor!' gulped Kevin without thinking. 'I was just looking for my brother. Honest!'

Grumpy lifted him higher and shook him. At that, Maureen emerged from her hiding-place in fury and started to hammer at him with her fists. 'Let him go, you big bully! You're hurting him!'

Grumpy swung around. 'Another one, is it? Well, you two can just come with us and behave yourselves. Toss me that rope there, Aidan.'

Stubble, who was on top of the wall, threw down the rope he had been carrying and Grumpy deftly wound it around the two children so that they were captive, back to back. 'Now let's see you get out of that one! Any more of you out there?'

'No!' shouted Kevin.

Grumpy just pulled the rope tighter and secured it to the ladder. 'There! You'll not be able to reach that, young fellow. You two can wait here until we see to the rest of the little gang.'

Grumpy disappeared up the ladder, and as he vanished Maeve crept out of the bush.

'Quick!' whispered Maureen. 'Untie the rope from the ladder first.'

Maeve began pulling at the rope but it was tight and her fingers were small.

'Hurry! They'll be back in a minute.'

They could hear the sounds of grunts and loud scraping noises from the other side of the wall, then one final crash.

'They're pulling the cover over Teddy and Liam!' wailed Kevin. 'They'll be killed!'

'Ssh!' ordered Maeve. 'I've got it!' and she pulled the rope clear of the ladder and began to unravel the rope from Kevin's shoulders. 'Nearly there. Just keep still.'

The rope came clear and Maeve began to attack Maureen's bonds. Just as the latter had wriggled free there came a shout from the wall, 'Hey, those kids are getting away. You there, stop!'

'Not on your life!' yelled back Maeve. 'Quick, back to the house and get Dad!'

The three children flew out of the old mill building and up the side of the hill, thankful now that they still had bare feet. Behind them they could hear the men panting as they tried to catch up, but as luck would have it Grumpy had changed his town shoes for heavy wellingtons and could not move quickly. Maeve kept well ahead of the other two and did not stop running until she had burst into the kitchen — only to come to a dismayed halt as she saw the room empty and a note on the table.

'Oh, no! They've gone into Foxford to collect a car battery for Dad, while Uncle Con's car was here. They won't be back for hours! What are we going to do?'

'Have you a neighbour with a phone?' asked Maureen. 'I think we'd better call the guards.'

'Not for a couple of miles,' answered Maeve. 'I just don't know what to do! Do you really think Teddy and Liam are in danger?'

'They were in the steps,' said Kevin, sobbing. 'There wasn't any other hiding-place. They're there still.'

'I'm sure they're okay,' soothed Maureen. 'They won't be very comfortable but they will be able to crouch under that stone thing. All the same, we have to get help.'

'You're not going anywhere!' panted a very angry voice as the door swung open. 'This is as far as you go.'

It was Grumpy! Behind him, an equally breathless and angry Stubble barred the exit.

'This time I'll tie them!' announced Stubble, glaring at Maeve. 'She won't be letting them go a second time.'

'You wait till my Dad catches you!' retorted Maeve furiously, aiming a kick at Stubble as he tried to catch her. He pushed her sharply towards the wall, and as she lost her balance he passed the rope over her head and around her shoulders, pulling it so tight that she began to cough. Maureen was next and she did not dare to object while Grumpy was standing there looking so fierce. Kevin was last, and finally Stubble wound the rope around the three of them several times so that they were standing in a triangle with their backs facing inwards. They could not move without collapsing in a heap.

'You'll be safe now,' decided Stubble. 'Just in case, we'll lock the door! Your mum and dad will find the key in the yard, but by that time we'll be gone!'

The children heard the key click in the lock, then the clink as it landed among the cobblestones.

'Gone!' said Kevin. 'I hope the folks won't be long.'

'I'm scared,' admitted Maeve. 'I wish we had never followed them.'

'I'm going to get tired standing like this,' said Maureen. 'Let's try and sit down. If we all let our feet slide outwards at the same time, we might be able to get down to the floor.'

With much shuffling and wriggling they reached floor level at last and settled down to wait for rescue to come.

Teddy and Liam waited a good ten minutes before deciding that it was safe to brave the tunnel again. They had heard the men return, but they had not realized what was happening. Now, as they retraced their steps down the tunnel, they found they were in total darkness. Liam switched on the torch, aiming it at the roof. The boys could see that the upper part of the tunnel was constructed of stone slabs set on end and leaning against each other, just like the floor in the round tower at Meelick.

'They must have gone now,' said Liam.

'Why is it so dark then?' answered Teddy.

'I'm going up the steps now.... Oh, no! They've pulled the slate cover right over and blocked us in.'

'I don't believe that. Let me see.'

'Nothing to see! Look — it's a solid lid. Not even a speck of light coming through, and we'll never move it on our own. It was hard enough for you four the other day, and you were working from the top. Maureen said you nearly couldn't pull it.'

'It was terribly heavy,' agreed Teddy. 'I'd say we're stuck.'

'There's only one thing to do then, isn't there? We'll go back to the ledge we were sitting on. Perhaps there's another way out.'

Teddy turned and began to feel his way back. He dragged himself up to the ledge and sat down wearily.

'What are we to do now? Wait till they dig us out?'

'Look at this!' was Liam's answer. He was flashing the torch around, gazing in fascination at the walls. 'We *are* in a round tower, Teddy. That ledge is only the last step up into it. It's exactly the same as the one at Meelick. That's what he meant by a tower at the end of the tunnel.'

'So the missing round tower really exists,' said Teddy. 'A round tower buried in a mountain!'

Liam shone the torch upwards. About six metres over their heads was the remnant of a once corbelled ceiling, now pierced with jagged rocks.

'The top fell in. This must be all that is left. I guess it fell in centuries ago, and then when there was a landslide the rubble from the fall covered it over and it was forgotten.'

'Are you quite sure it's a tower?'

'You've only got to look at the walls. That's the door up

79

there, that oval shape. There's probably even a grave-stone or two lying around somewhere.'

'*Or do Teddy!*' uttered Teddy mournfully. 'I don't feel quite so sorry for Gricour now. It looks like I'm going to be the next one!'

'This would have been under the room with the entrance door,' said Liam, 'so this would have been a cellar. Round towers *did* sometimes have escape tunnels — now we have proof.'

'Why would the escape lead to a mill?' protested Teddy.

'The mill wouldn't have been there when the tower was built. It was probably built on the ruins of a farmhouse, or one of the outbuildings of a monastery. That monastery is long gone now, just like Meelick. Only a few stones remain here and there, and they would have been used in the mill buildings.'

'Some consolation knowing all that when we are buried alive!' was Teddy's comment.

'Oh, that roof is sound. We're safe here for a while. Never you fear — the others will help us out later.'

'Of course,' said Teddy, becoming more cheerful. 'It all makes sense now. The last landslide diverted the river and flooded the passage, so they walled up the access room. And that's why Grumpy's great-grandfather couldn't get in. But why did he want to get in? And why does Grumpy want to get in so badly? What's in here that is so important?'

Liam shone the torch around the walls again, lingering on some of the larger niches. The surface was of large dressed stones, and most of the lower stones still pre-sented a smooth close-fitting face. Higher up, where part

80

of the roof had fallen and jammed in on itself, there were occasional hollows in the stones where the torch beam could not penetrate. Higher again, the space which had once been the entrance was blocked with earth and rubble.

'I can't see any hiding-place except those gaps up there,' said Liam. 'But I don't see how anyone could have climbed up there to hide anything.'

'How about the floor? Shine it round our feet. There might be a trapdoor down to another level.'

'I doubt it,' replied Liam. 'It would be flooded anyway even if there was one.' However he flashed the torch around, just in case. 'Nothing.'

'Wait!' ordered Teddy. 'Shine it over there again.'

Liam directed the beam towards the wall opposite the steps and Teddy followed the ray. 'Keep it shining here. There's a kind of gap under the wall.' He knelt down and slipped his fingers in.

'Jackpot! There *is* something here.' He pulled hard and an old cracked leather case, wreathed with strands of cobwebs and scraps of rotten cloth, slid out. 'I've found something, whatever it is!'

Liam dropped to his knees and the two boys tried to prise the case open. The leather had long since perished and the lid had jammed tight shut. They pulled at it with all their strength, but it was clear that the case would have to be cut open.

'For all the good it will do us!' observed Teddy. 'No doubt we'll be buried along with it. Once they start digging on the outside that lot could come down.'

'Don't give up hope,' said Liam. 'They're after the case too, so they won't be in that much of a hurry to bury it. They will dig through without any problem. The surface is just loose stones.'

'That's what you think!' retorted Teddy. 'It gives me the creeps to look at that roof. Let's go and wait in the tunnel now. At least *that* roof is intact.'

'And catch pneumonia instead!' scoffed Liam. 'I'm not standing in that freezing water, thank you!'

The boys fell into a gloomy silence. An hour passed before it occurred to Teddy to check his watch to see how long they had been underground, but the water had got into it, and the hands had stuck at midday.

'Great!' he said. 'Here we are, stuck for ever in a tunnel nobody even knows exists. The others will think we have drowned.'

'Not Kevin,' asserted Liam, remembering how stubborn Kevin could be when he believed in something. 'He won't give up until he has the slab moved. And neither will Maureen. The men must be still up there, and that's why we haven't been rescued.'

'They'd better get cracking soon,' declared Teddy. 'The batteries are going.'

'That's just great!' agreed Liam. 'Turn it off, in case we need it later.'

Teddy switched the torch off and their eyes blinked in the new darkness. A very faint phosphorescence was still thrown off by the tunnel roof, but it was not sufficient to light up the utter blackness.

'What did they do when the Titanic went down?' asked Teddy. 'Sing hymns, wasn't it?'

'What's the Titanic...?' began Liam, but he was stopped by Teddy who suddenly shouted, 'Wait!' and then leapt to his feet, simultaneously switching on the torch and directing the beam down the passage. Was it his imagination or could he hear a scraping noise?

Then they both heard it — the most welcome sound in the world — Kevin's voice calling, 'Teddy! Liam! Are you in there? Talk to us!'

Liam went skidding down the steps into the water and then raced down the tunnel. Teddy grabbed the case and went down the steps after him. He tripped, the torch went flying out of his hand and he landed full length in the water. His hand caught Liam's ankle as he fell, and Liam too went sprawling. Choking and spitting the foul water out again, the two boys scrambled to their feet and floundered as fast as they could to the steps beneath the slate cover. Chinks of light showed round the edges.

Kevin's voice was still calling, 'Teddy! Answer me!'

'We're here!' gasped Liam. 'Can you get us out?'

'We're trying to move the stone,' called Maeve, 'but it's heavy. Can you help from down there?'

'Sure thing!' said Liam. He could see several sets of fingers now, pulling at one of the edges. Lifting up the palms of his hands, he added his strength. The stone moved slightly.

'Come on, Teddy!' urged Liam. 'Quick ... the sooner we get out the better.'

Teddy let go of the case and began to push too. Slowly the stone slid aside, and the faces of Maureen, Kevin and Maeve appeared.

'Hurry,' ordered Maureen. 'They've started digging up the hillside. They have all sorts of queer stuff up there — I think they are going to blow a hole in the mountain.'

The boys scrambled out of the opening, Teddy retrieving his case quickly. He wasn't going to leave it behind now!

'Up the rope now,' said Maeve. 'Let's get out of here. We left a note at the house, so the parents should be soon after us.'

One after the other, the children swarmed up the rope, which Maeve had secured once more, and over the wall of the house. The five of them raced out of the mill building and up the hillside on the other side of the valley. Reaching the summit of the hill, they sank down one by one to catch their breaths.

They could see the two men quite clearly now. Grumpy was attaching a line to a large box which he had half wedged in the ground. Stubble stood alongside, a smaller box in his hands. As the children watched them, Stubble nodded and began to pick up the tools. Grumpy straightened up and brushed down the knees of his trousers, then he too began to collect up the equipment. They came back downhill to the mill, and Stubble gave his tools to Grumpy so that he could carry the ladder. The two men started up the slope towards the children, staggering under their loads.

'We'd better get out of here,' said Kevin.

'They can't see us,' said Liam. 'Let's wait and watch them.'

Grumpy and Stubble did not try to reach the hilltop however. They settled themselves about half way up and then Stubble let the ladder fall.

'This is far enough. We'll take a rest here and let the lot blow. Then we wait a few minutes for the dust to clear.'

Maeve nudged Maureen. Stubble's voice had carried quite clearly up the slope, and the children flattened themselves out in case the two men should look upwards.

'Do they realize how dangerous that is?' hissed

Maureen to Liam. 'They'll cause another landslide.'

'Obviously they don't care. They just want whatever is in the tower.'

'And we've got it!' said Teddy. 'If they only knew...'

'SSSH!' urged Maureen.

'What about the other kids?' asked Grumpy.

'They'll be all right. It's only a small charge. They'll be in those bushes round the house somewhere.'

'Good thing you covered that old hole,' said Grumpy, 'or they might have gone in there to hide.'

'No chance. I could see water at the bottom. It must have filled in long ago .... Now I'm going to let it go, just in case those other three get free and come back.'

He held out a small box and Teddy craned his neck to see. Grumpy was now standing up, gazing at the mountain side.

'Ready?'

'Let it go!'

Stubble pushed the button, and for a second the children thought nothing had happened. Then a little puff of dust rose from the slope above the mill — and all of a sudden a shower of small stones and shingle came rolling down the hillside. For a split second there was an image of a tall stone wall inside the hole, then more stones came rolling down. Somewhere beneath them the ground shook, and all of a sudden Grumpy lost his balance and fell heavily, his foot splaying awkwardly beneath him. He gave one yell of surprise.

'Get me up! I've hurt my leg!'

Stubble scrambled down the slope and bent to look at him. Then he looked up and caught sight of the children on the hilltop.

'Hey, you lot! Get down here and help us!'

'Serve him right!' uttered Maeve rudely, but Maureen and Liam had already started down to help. Teddy followed grudgingly, but not before he had handed the case to Kevin.

'Get back to the house and hide that!' he whispered. 'We're not going to lose it now.'

Kevin melted away up the track.

'His leg is broken,' announced Liam, after one quick glance. 'You can see the way it's sticking out. He won't be able to walk up the hill.'

'You can't leave me here,' wailed Grumpy.

'You'll have to stay here until we get help,' said Maureen. 'You can't move a person with a broken leg.'

'Look at the mountain!' yelled Maeve suddenly, adding in an awed voice. 'It's a good thing we got out of the way in time!'

As they watched, a huge slice of the mountain detached itself from the face, seemed to hover momentarily over the valley, then crashed into the river. A small shower of pebbles followed, then all was silence. The pall of dust cleared gradually, revealing the extent of the damage. The mill and outbuildings had completely vanished under the debris, and the river-bed was choked to over-flowing. Before their eyes a little trickle of silver came snaking through the rocks and around the old mill site.

'The river has gone back to its original bed,' announced Maeve. 'It's as though the mill and the round tower and everything else never existed.'

8   Secret of the Lost Tower

'What's going on? Is everything all right?' called Con, racing over the brow of the hill followed by his brother-in-law. 'Maureen, are you there?'

'We're all here!' shouted Teddy. 'Right here, Dad!'

Stubble rose hurriedly to his feet, but the only escape was barred by Con and Ed.

'This man tried to kill us!' yelled Teddy. 'Stop him!'

'Just a minute, there,' said Con sternly. 'You, who are you?'

'I'm Professor Quinn's assistant,' babbled Stubble, quite unnerved by the effect of the explosion. 'I have to be off!'

'You sit down right there,' ordered Ed. 'Nobody is going anywhere until someone tells us what happened.'

'They blew up the mountain!' shouted Maeve indignantly. 'OUR mountain, Dad!'

'I've got a broken leg,' moaned Grumpy. 'I'm sure it's a compound fracture.'

'It seems strange things have been going on,' said Ed sternly. 'First of all we got your note, Maeve ...'

'Oh, that ...' explained Maureen to Teddy and Liam. 'We left a note to tell them about your hiding in the well-shaft and how these men tied us up.'

'In the kitchen,' put in Maeve. 'But Kevin managed to wriggle free and untie us. We had to break a window to get out because the door was locked and we couldn't get the sash to move.'

'Your mother has called the guards,' said Ed. 'They'll be here shortly and take care of these two characters. She phoned UCD as well, Maureen — and you were quite right. The real Professor Quinn is there at this very moment, and hasn't been in Mayo for the past two years. Good thinking to put that in your note! Now what about this well-shaft?'

'It wasn't a well-shaft!' burst out Teddy. 'It was a tunnel after all. It led into a tower and we were trapped in there.'

'You didn't happen to find anything in there, I suppose?' asked Grumpy casually.

'Oh, nothing of importance!' replied Liam airily. 'Just an old leather case. I imagine the police have it by now.'

Grumpy made a lunge at him, but the pain in his leg caught him and he fell back in fury. 'You'll pay for this!'

'Here come the guards now,' announced Maeve.

Two policeman, accompanied by Kevin, had just appeared at the far end of the track.

'Glad to see you!' said Con. 'It appears that these men are up to no good, and one of them has ended up breaking his leg.'

'Have to get a stretcher for him,' said the taller of the two guards. 'Would you go and phone the garda station, Mr. McGrath? We'll stay here with these two until help arrives.'

'Of course . . . come on, kids, we'll get back to the house and sort you out. Your mothers will be worried sick about you, and goodness only knows what yours will say when she sees you've fallen in again, Teddy!'

Later that afternoon, after Teddy and Liam had been

88

given dry clothing and mugs of hot tea and were beginning to feel human again, Kevin and the girls gathered around the kitchen table, watching as Ed attacked the leather with a saw. The material was thick and completely rigid and it was obvious that nothing less would break through it. The two police officers, who had arrived shortly beforehand to take statements from the children, now sat in two kitchen chairs, as eager as the rest to see the contents of the case.

'Let me have a turn,' suggested Con after a while, 'I'm more of a hand with a saw than you are, Ed.'

He took the tool and began working on the top where Ed had left off. 'I've pierced it. We'll be through in a moment now .... Yes, it's giving! Look, I can nearly rip this with my fingers now.'

Sure enough, when the reinforced corners had been broached, the centre panel, which was quite thin, ripped straight across as Con pulled it. He forced the lid backwards and reached into the case. The contents had been wrapped in sacking, but this disintegrated as soon as it was touched and a cloud of dust rose into the air. Inside the sacking was a second layer of material, bleached of all colour by age.

'I think this must have been silk once,' said Con. 'It feels very soft.'

He peeled back the layers, rubbing his fingers to release the rotten material which kept adhering to them. Finally the contents were revealed — and every person in the room was standing over the case so as not to miss the moment when Con reverently lifted them out.

'A lunula!' exclaimed Ed. 'And a torque ... and another lunula! Do you realize just what this is?'

'Jewellery!' said Kevin brightly. 'Old jewellery!'

'This isn't just old jewellery,' said Ed. 'This is the finest collection I've ever seen! Three torques, two lunulae and two sun discs! They were all Bronze Age ornaments. Do you know how old they are?'

'A thousand years,' ventured Maeve.

'At least three thousand, perhaps more!' answered Ed. He held one of the torques up to the light. 'And still as beautiful as ever! These would have been worn by a great lady in Germany or Italy or perhaps even further away. The goldsmiths in those days were exporting their work all over Europe. Irish gold was highly prized.'

The torque was just like a twisted rope, and very heavy. He passed it over to one of the guards, who weighed it across his hand.

'The great lady wouldn't have run far with this on!' he laughed.

'What were the lunulas and sun discs?' asked Teddy. 'Were they kinds of necklace too?'

'Lunulae,' corrected Ed. 'Yes. The lunula was a flat necklace shaped like a moon in the first quarter, and the sun disc might have been worn as a pendant. Look at the engravings on this!'

'Why did the men want them so badly?' asked Maureen. 'Are they so very valuable?'

'Priceless. They must have been really desperate to go to the lengths they did. You children were lucky to escape without injury.'

'How did the men know how to find the treasure?' asked Con. 'It was well hidden in the mountain.'

'Grumpy — I mean, the man who called himself Professor Quinn — had a map,' explained Maureen. 'His great-grandfather hid the case a long time ago, before the last landslide when the river changed course and flooded the access tunnel. He may have stolen the collection originally, maybe from a museum, and decided to hide it until the crime was forgotten and he could try to sell it. But he didn't bargain on the landslide and the tunnel being blocked, and soon after that he became ill and never did get back to claim it. He had a map, a sketch which he had copied from an old book. Luckily, the author's name was on the copy and we got hold of the original, in Castlebar. To make it harder for anyone other than himself to come back and find it, he didn't actually record the location of the "tower" on the same page.'

'So there were two treasures,' said Liam. 'The one the monk originally left, and the treasure that Grumpy's great-grandfather left.'

'I think they were the same treasure,' Teddy suggested. 'Maybe Grumpy's relation didn't steal it. He found it, and packed it in a case to bring it away, but someone or something must have stopped him, and he never got back to collect it again.'

'Why did he hide it?' asked Kevin. 'If he didn't steal it in the first place, he could have just taken it.'

'We'll never know,' said Maureen. 'Maybe he had an accomplice and was trying to hide it from *him*. Certainly the case is quite modern. It couldn't possibly have belonged to the monk.'

'If he had only known that the water level had got lower again over the years and he could have just walked in!' exclaimed Maeve. 'I almost feel sorry for him.'

'And did the old map tell you how to come here?' asked Con.

'No, we checked the ordnance survey maps,' Maureen explained. 'The change in the river course showed up clearly, as one set was made before the landslide and one after. Grumpy and Stubble clued in at the same time as we did — except they were one step ahead. They had worked out that the tower could be buried under the landslide.'

'I wonder was there ever a monastery there?' wondered Ed. 'We'll never know now. It would be far too dangerous to excavate there. The entire valley could end up buried next time!'

'I think the mill might have been built on the ruins of a monastery,' said Teddy. 'The tunnel would have been the only remaining part of the original buildings. That and the buried tower, of course.'

'The mill owners may not have even known it was a round tower,' said Maeve. 'They might have just thought it was an underground store-room.'

'Like an ice-house,' added Maureen. 'They were round too.'

'So why was the mill abandoned?' asked Ed.

'Technology,' Con replied. 'And the fact that the site was unstable. They would never have known when there would be another landslide. There must have been constant little ones.'

'What a silly place to put a round tower anyway!' snorted Maeve. 'They should have known better!'

'In those days they weren't great geologists,' answered Ed. 'And we don't know what the landscape was like. It could very likely have been built in the middle of a plain and there could have been an earthquake which threw up the mountain behind the tower. We could spend a lifetime wondering about it and get no nearer to the reason.'

'Of course there is always the possibility that the tower had nothing to do with a monastery,' said Con. 'The usual explanation for the towers is they were used as a refuge or a storage place for valuables for the monks who lived in the monastery beside it. But some authorities think the towers were there long before, and the monks just built their monasteries next door because it was convenient. One theory is that they could have been used as observatories for primitive astronomers. Another that they were places where holy men could shut themselves away from the world and meditate.'

'As you said, Ed,' commented Eileen, 'we could spend a lifetime wondering about it. Now I think Sile and I should confer, and see how we can keep the children out of any more mischief!'

'How about coming down to the garda station with us and handing over the case officially to the superintendant?' suggested the older guard. 'That should keep you all out of trouble for a while.'

The children squeezed into the back seat of the car and the guards took their places in front.

'Have the baddies gone?' asked Kevin.

'Long since. One of them is safely tucked up in hospital and the other one is down town right now making a statement.'

'Who does the gold go to?' asked Teddy.

'The state, I suppose,' answered the younger guard.

'In that case,' decided Teddy, 'I'll just have to work on becoming President!'

Notes for Teachers

Treasure trove! How exciting it sounds, conjuring up visions of pirates and chests of gold doubloons, and how rarely we expect to come across it in real life. But there *is* treasure buried in Ireland. In the National Museum of Ireland, in Dublin, you can see some of the magnificent treasure, buried centuries ago, that was eventually discovered. The Ardagh chalice, the Derrynaflan chalice, the Shrine of St. Patrick are just a few. And the largest known horde of Viking gold, weighing over ten pounds, was found on a small island on the River Shannon. Sadly, it was melted down by people who didn't realize its value.

This should remind us all of an important point: 'Treasure' should only be excavated by an expert. Often the exact spot in which it is found, the soil around it, its condition, are vital clues which only a trained archalologist can interpret.

Suggestions for projects: Treasures of the past — their discovery and restoration; lost or missing treasure — where might it be found (substantiated by research into wealthy monastic foundations which were sacked or destroyed); the round towers of Ireland — their origins and histories; the myths and legends of a locality — have they any foundation in fact; how effective are our laws in safeguarding treasure trove for the nation; gold mining in Ireland (in *The Children of the Forge,* Tom McCaughren recalls the Wicklow gold rush of 1798); craftsmanship in Irish gold jewellery.

Jo Ann Galligan

Jo Ann Galligan was born in New Zealand, where her first poem was broadcast on local radio when she was six years old. Since then she has written many poems and short stories, some of which have appeared in Connacht newspapers. She has also written several hymns for performance in local churches.

Since 1978 she has lived on a small holding in Mayo with her Irish husband Frank and their three children, David, Cathleen and Helen. She works part-time as a church organist and teacher, and her spare time is spent bee-keeping, rearing poultry, growing vegetables, and writing.

This is her second book for The Children's Press. Her first, *Mystery at Rinn Mor,* was published in November 1985.

Hawthorn

is a new imprint for The Children's Press and will appear on *historical* fiction. The first two titles are:

1 *A Foster Son for a King* Nicholas Furlong. The Norman invasion of Ireland, seen through the eyes of the Welsh boy, Gwynn, who becomes Dermot Mac-Murrough's foster son.

2 *Murtagh and the Vikings* Roger Chatterton Newman. The first Viking raid on Rathlin Island. Murtagh is captured and brought to Norway, where he has many adventures.

Acorn

Adventure fiction for 9 to 12 year olds, in Irish settings.

1 *Robbers in the House* Carolyn Swift
2 *Robbers in the Hills* Carolyn Swift
3 *The Big Push* Joe O'Donnell
4 *Legend of the Golden Key* Tom McCaughren
5 *Robbers in the Town* Carolyn Swift
6 *Legend of the Phantom Highwayman*
Tom McCaughren
7 *Legend of the Corrib King* Tom McCaughren
8 *Robbers in the Theatre* Carolyn Swift
9 *Mystery at Rinn Mor* Jo Ann Galligan
10 *Children of the Forge* Tom McCaughren
11 *The Black Dog* Tony Hickey
12 *The Mystery of the Lost Tower* Jo Ann Galligan

Also by The Children's Press
Silas Rat Dermot O'Donovan
The Matchless Mice's Adventure Tony Hickey
The Matchless Mice in Space Tony Hickey
The Grey Goose of Kilnevin (paperback) Patricia Lynch